What They're Saying about
Exploring Colorado Wineries

"Fortunately for wine-lovers everywhere, Paula Mitchell knows the story and like an alchemist she has turned her knowledge and affection for Colorado's wine industry into a delightful book. Mitchell takes readers on a tour of the people, places and grapes that make Colorado such a fascinating place to make and enjoy wine. Like finding the just-right Reidel glass, this well-researched and engaging book is the perfect accompaniment to a trip through Colorado wine country."
 – Dave Buchanan, Wine Writer, *The Daily Sentinel*

"In *Exploring Colorado Wineries,* Paula Mitchell introduces the reader to the joys of wine tasting and touring in the Centennial State while taking out some of the mystery and intimidation sometimes associated with tasting, sampling and enjoying wine. Written simply, this guide has something for the newcomer as well as the more experienced sommelier."
 – Jim Clark, CDME, President & CEO, Fort Collins Convention
  and Visitors Bureau

"A great tool to help you discover the fast-growing Colorado wine industry. Along with winery profiles, their locations and maps, the bonus of this guidebook is a Wine Tasting 101 with tips for truly tasting your next glass of wine, and learning about grape varieties and wine terminology. I love the journal section with each winery for tasting notes."
 – Sandie Cooper, Administrator, Colorado Association for
  Viticulture and Enology (CAVE)

"Paula Mitchell's new book is an indispensable guide to exploring America's Wild West Of Wine! It will help you discover Colorado's wine country as well as urban wine tasting destinations. This handy book also includes practical how-to information that is sure to help you increase your pure enjoyment of wine!"
 – Christopher J. Davies, Editor and Co-Founder,
  Wine Country International® magazine

"An incredible resource for newcomers to Colorado wines."
 – Shawn C. Miller, Publisher, *Denver Life Mago*

"*Exploring Colorado Wineries* is a great resource for wine lovers or those who are just new to the appreciation of wine. This guide will help take you through the wine regions of Colorado with great tips for enjoying this growing culinary industry in Colorado. The book will become your must have companion with maps to wineries, tasting pointers and space to make your own notes as you sip your way along."
   – Kelli Hepler, Coordinator, Delta County Tourism Cabinet

"What fun to discover the wines of Colorado in this winery guide of the state. Learn about places that are part of our state with explanations of each wine."
   – Pat Miller aka the Gabby Gourmet, author of *The Gabby Gourmet Restaurant Guides*

"*Exploring Colorado Wineries* is a full-bodied guide to understanding the state's rich assets including vineyards, tasting rooms, and individual wines. This book is an essential resource for anyone seeking insight into Colorado's well-rounded wine culture."
   – John Brackney, President & CEO, South Metro Denver Chamber of Commerce

"A very informative guidebook covering all of the Colorado Wineries. A good read for both newcomers to wine and seasoned tasters. Especially great resource to visitors to the State who are not aware of just how many great wineries we have in Colorado. Having moved here from California, I was one of those people. This guidebook will now be part of my library."
   – Floyd O'Neil, Events Director, iManitou Colorado Wine Festival

"You've picked a wonderful book about Colorado wine. Now bring the book and come get a "taste" of the real Wine Country experience."
   – Barb Bowman, Division Manager, Grand Junction Visitor and Convention Bureau

"A useful companion for people wanting to visit Colorado wineries, it's especially helpful for those who are just starting in their exploration of the vine and grape."
   – Ed Sealover, author of *Mountain Brew: A Guide to Colorado's Breweries*

"As a lifelong resident of Western Colorado it was my pleasure to review *Exploring Colorado Wineries* by Paula Mitchell. I would hope that the reader gets as much enjoyment and information from it as I did."
   – *Roger Granat, Palisade, Colorado*

"Delta County is no longer Colorado's best kept secret. With *Exploring Colorado Wineries*, Paula Mitchell shines the light on our little corner of the state. Use this book as your guide to locating our great boutique wineries. Along the way you can also savor locally grown fruits and vegetables, beautiful works of art and some incredible mountain views!"
   – Pat Sunderland, Managing Editor, *Delta County Independent*

"Durango prides itself on being the "City of Brewerly Love" with 4 microbreweries in our quintessential Southwestern Colorado city. The recent culinary attention comes from the increased quality of wines, tasting rooms and wineries in the region. Colorado now challenges some of the finest California vintners. It's refreshing to see a book that gives credit to the quality wineries that call Colorado home."
   – Anne Klein, Public Relations, Durango Area Tourism Office

Exploring
Colorado
Wineries

Guidebook & Journal

Explore and
Enjoy!

Paula Mitchell

Summit Mesa Publishing

Exploring Colorado Wineries: Guidebook & Journal
By Paula Mitchell

Disclaimer: All information contained in this book is deemed to be current as of the date of this publication.

Published by

⌐ Summit Mesa Publishing

P.O. Box 2134
Littleton, Colorado 80161

Cover and Interior Layout by Nick Zelinger, www.NZGraphics.com

ISBN: 978-0-9851508-0-8

Library of Congress Control Number: 2012932506

First Edition 2012

Printed in Korea

Visit www.ExploringColoradoWineries.com (for print or ebook purchases)

To my husband Jim...
for all the times I said "Can you help me?"
and you did!
Thanks for your thoughts, support and encouragement
both on the book and in life.

Contents

WINE REGIONS

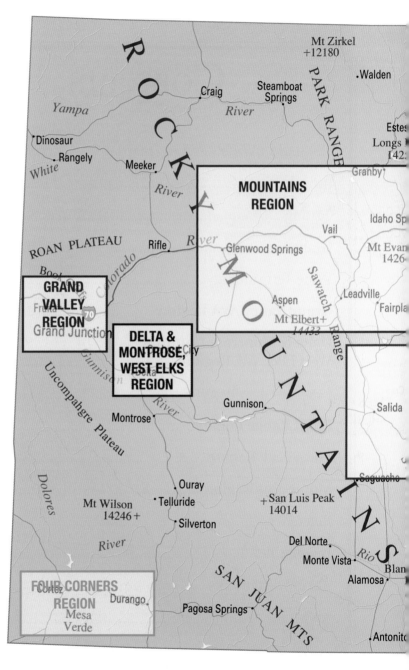

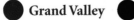 **Grand Valley**  **Delta & Montrose, West Elks**   Four Corners

OF COLORADO

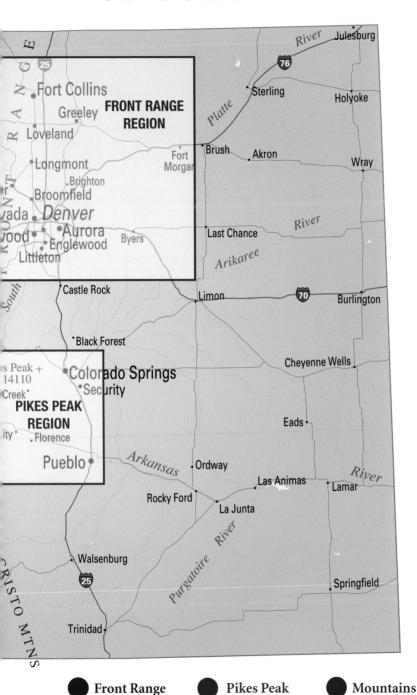

Front Range **Pikes Peak** **Mountains**

INTRODUCTION

I t's hard to believe I even like wine, since my first tasting experience was my father's homemade dandelion wine. Yuck! Next came an apple jug wine, yuck again! Fortunately, my wine appreciation and experiences have vastly improved over the years. While I am not a sommelier or an oenologist, I have gained quite a bit of wine knowledge by tasting, reading and keeping notes. A combined interest in wine and love of Colorado, my home state, has resulted in this guidebook.

The primary goal of *Exploring Colorado Wineries* is assisting you in discovering all of Colorado's wineries and their wines. As I wrote the book and talked to family, friends and colleagues, it became apparent that most Coloradoans are unaware of the number of wineries and tasting rooms throughout the state and the high quality of wines produced here. Whether you are just beginning your wine education, a wine expert or someone in between, I hope this guidebook can help you discover and explore Colorado's wineries and tasting rooms, and you too can begin to savor their wines!

A Brief History of Colorado Wineries...

Grapes have been grown and wine has been made in Colorado since the 1860s. When the Ute Indians were evacuated from the Grand Valley region (near present-day Grand Junction and Palisade) in the mid-1880s, fruit trees and grapevine stock were brought into this area, and home-fermented wine was made for personal consumption. In the late 19th century, Italian immigrants arrived in the area and sought out available wine. It was at this time that both grape vines and fruit trees really began to flourish on the Western Slope.

Then came the Women's Christian Temperance Union and Prohibition. Due to these movements, the majority of grape vines were uprooted and replaced with only fruit trees. Although many farmers were permitted to make 40 gallons of "grape juice" for their personal consumption, fruit became the main agricultural product on the Western Slope.

It wasn't until the late 1960s when Dr. Gerald and Mary Ivancie along with Jim and Ann Seewald began developing in the Grand Valley area, what is now Colorado's present-day wine industry. In 1980, Jim Seewald and others formed a winery called Colorado Mountain Vineyards. The name has changed to Colorado Cellars, but it is Colorado's oldest winery still in operation today.

By the early 1990s many other wineries were beginning to establish themselves. Two American Viticultural Areas (AVA) were designated: Grand Valley in 1991 and West Elks in 2001. Today, the Colorado wine industry continues to expand and develop statewide. *Exploring Colorado Wineries* provides you with Colorado's current winery operations.

How to Use the Book...

The first section of the book provides general wine information, including **Tasting, Grape Varieties** and **Wine Terminology**. If you are not familiar with the tasting process or need a little refresher, these pages review the basics, provide wine-related vocabulary and explain how my wine studies began. **The Grape Varieties** section contains information on the grapes commonly grown in Colorado and their typical tastes. A glossary of frequently used **Wine Terminology** can help you increase and broaden your wine vocabulary. So if you hear someone say, "This wine tastes grassy," you won't be tempted to look in your wine glass for floating pieces of grass but will know it's a word used to describe an herbal taste in a wine!

Colorado is typically divided into six wine regions: Grand Valley AVA, Delta and Montrose County and West Elks AVA, Four Corners Region, the Front Range, Pikes Peak area and the Mountains. For easy reference, I have used that system, color-coded each region and included an overall map. The wineries in each region are listed in alphabetical order. Each winery's page contains contact and tasting room information, the wines produced, a message from the owner and easy-to-follow directions. (Note: Information is accurate as of January, 2012.)

Because I am getting to the age when "if I don't write it down, I won't remember it," I have included a **Notes** section on each winery's page. I highly recommend you jot down a few notes to help remember the wineries and their wines. Touring wineries with my children was always about compromise (keeping them happy while I enjoyed myself!), so I have included the **What Else To See & Do** sections for each region, listing a few interesting places to visit. Learn more at local Chambers of Commerce, visitors bureaus and www.colorado.com.

*Exploring Colorado Winerie*s is all about reading, tasting, learning, discovering and exploring Colorado's wineries. I hope you enjoy your adventure! And please remember to drink and drive responsibly.

Explore and Enjoy!

Paula Mitchell

TASTING

To truly know a grape or a wine is to taste it! What could be more fun? Books are helpful and informative, and I would highly recommend reading a few on the subject, but nothing surpasses first-hand experience. So how should you begin and become an expert? Or, at least give it a good try. Here's how I began.

I first created a "Tasting Journal" (see more information below) so I could keep notes and impressions about the wines I sampled. A journal can range from a simple, small notebook to an extensive binder for keeping labels and meticulous details. However you want to organize yourself is fine; just take notes.

Which wines should you try first? Start with something familiar. Chardonnay had been my wine of choice for years, so I bought bottles of Old World and New World Chardonnay and began to taste and compare their characteristics. Once comfortable with the process, I began to branch out and try other common white wines. I would pick a particular grape, learn about it and taste bottles from several different regions and/or countries. From my experiences, I discovered that comparing three to five wines at a time worked best. When I gained enough knowledge about that grape, I would try another, using the same methodology. After learning about several white wines, I applied the process to reds.

Having a basic knowledge of a particular grape's taste profile, it's then fun to sample several different grapes at the same time, comparing them and testing your new-found skills. An example would be tasting a flight of whites (Chardonnay, Sauvignon Blanc, Pinot Grigio and Riesling) or reds (Pinot Noir, Syrah, Merlot and Cabernet Sauvignon). You could also increase your proficiency by tasting and comparing the same grape from a Colorado winery versus California, Washington and Oregon.

My Personal Tasting Journal Includes...

- Basic information about the wine: type, region, vineyard, vintage
- Purchase information: where and when I bought it, cost
- Color of the wine
- Aromas I detected
- Tastes (be as specific as possible)
- Grade (using a scale of 1-10 or A-F)
- What I liked or didn't like about the wine (be descriptive)
- Date

Tasting Order...

It's important to taste wine in a particular order. You don't want to drink a red wine before a white, or a sweet before a dry, as that can alter your perceived taste of the wine. The standard rules are:

- Drink white wines before red wines (Chardonnay before a Cabernet)
- Sample delicate wines before strong wines (Pinot Noir before Merlot before Zinfandel)
- Taste dry wines before sweet wines before dessert wines (Sauvignon Blanc before Riesling before Port)

Tasting Procedure: The Five S's...

You have your tasting method decided and your trusty notebook in hand, so what is the proper tasting process? By following the steps below while tasting a few wines, you will become a pro in no time! A piece of advice—only fill the glass with about 1" of wine for tasting. That will give you enough to smell, taste and critique without spilling as you swirl.

SEE: To gauge a wine's color, tip the glass slightly and hold a white sheet of paper or napkin behind the glass. Is this typically the wine's color pigmentation? The more you try various wines, you will notice how the color can differ. Whites can range from almost clear to a deep gold. Reds range from a purple hue to ruby to brown. As white wines age, they gain color. For reds the opposite is true; they lose color or brilliance over time.

Traditional Colors in Wine...

Whites:		Reds:	
	clear		purple
	pale yellow-green		red violet
	straw yellow		cherry red
	canary		red ruby
	yellow-gold		garnet
	gold		brick-red
	amber		red-brown

SWIRL: Swirling your glass introduces oxygen into the wine, which helps release the aromas or bouquet. Hold the stem of the glass with your thumb and first two fingers and slowly move it around in a circular motion two to three times. This is best done while keeping the glass flat on a table. This action brings the fragrances in the wine to the surface, allowing your nose to better perceive its various characteristics.

SMELL: Tilt the glass so you can literally stick your nose into the glass and take in a few breaths. Some people are shy about this procedure but just take two to three simple sniffs. There is no need to take one deep lungful as if it's your last gasping breath! What are some of the first, descriptive words that come to mind? Do you smell any fruit, earthy aromas, spices, plants, etc? The more you taste and experience different wines, the broader your "descriptive" vocabulary will become. Don't be embarrassed if you don't smell anything distinctly because some wines' aromas are harder to distinguish than others. After the wine is swirled, you may see "legs" or "tears" running down the inside of the glass. This phenomenon is still up for discussion, but know that there is a correlation between alcohol content and legs, not quality and legs.

SIP: Take a small sip...enough to fully experience the taste, without being a big gulp. Swish the wine around in your mouth for a few seconds. As you are doing this, what do you initially taste? What words come to your mind? Some major descriptors could be: types of fruits, earthy, floral or vegetal characteristics, various spices, herbs or plants. Next, think how the wine feels in your mouth. Does it seem light-, medium- or full-bodied? (think water, milk, cream) Does it have weight? Does the wine seem balanced between its fruit/acidity/tannin? Did anything stand out that is unpleasant?

SAVOR: After you have swallowed the sip, what else comes to your mind? Your first question should be "Did I like it?" Did your mouth pucker (tannin) or salivate (acidity)? Is there any aftertaste? Are there other flavors that reveal themselves, which you didn't experience during the sipping phase (complexity)? What other words can you use to describe the taste?

The most important outcome from the Five S's tasting procedure is...did YOU like it? No matter what other people may taste in the wine or say about it, how much the wine costs, who produced it, etc., the main point is whether you liked the wine or not. Are you interested in taking another sip, having a whole glass, buying a bottle, buying the winery?

Descriptive Words...

Kevin Zraly, a world-renowned wine author and educator, provides his students with a list of 500+ words to describe wine and what they might smell, taste and sense. This many options can be overwhelming, so here are the words that I generally use to describe a wine's characteristics.

acidity	complex	herbal	soft
aftertaste	corky	leather	smoky
aroma	crisp	light	spicy
astringent	delicate	mature	sweet
balanced	depth	mineral	tannin
big	dry	moldy	tar
bitter	earthy	musty	tart
body	finish	oaky	toasty
buttery	firm	nutty	tobacco
burnt rubber	floral flowers	pepper	vanilla
caramel	fresh	perfumed	vinegar
chewy	fruity	powerful	woody
chocolate	funky	pungent	yeasty
citrus	gamey	rich	young
color	grassy	short	yuck!

When You Think of Fruits, They Can be Broken Down into Several Basic Categories...

- Red fruits: strawberry, raspberry, red currant, cherry
- Black fruits: plums, blackcurrants, blackberry, black cherry
- Pome: apple, pear
- Drupe: peach, apricot, mango
- Tropical: pineapple, passion fruits
- Citrus: lemon, grapefruit

How to Read a Wine Label...

Reading an American (Colorado) wine bottle label is fairly simple compared with Old World wine labels. Below is the standard information contained on a label from the United States.

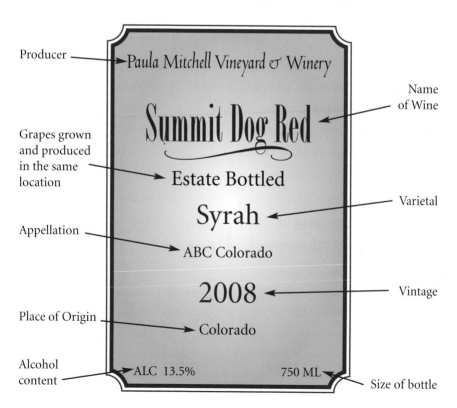

GRAPE VARIETIES

From Grape to Wine...

How do grapes turn into wine? It can be this simple: grow grapes, pick them, crush the grapes, put them into a container, and then wait. While this may be an oversimplification, it is the process typically used by a winemaker, who in turn then adds his/her own special touches and knowledge to create a wine unlike any other.

Winemakers either grow their own grapes or obtain grapes from another vineyard. Once the grapes have been selected and picked (a very crucial decision), they are crushed and put into containers for a designated period of time. Here, the yeasts mix with the natural sugar in the grape juice. (Yeasts are tiny one-celled organisms naturally occurring on the grape skin/stem and can also be added by the winemaker.) Fermentation takes place as the sugar converts to alcohol, which kills off the yeast. The grape juice is then commonly transferred into stainless steel tanks or oak barrels. The wine goes through a maturation phase lasting anywhere from a month to several years. It is then bottled and either ready to drink or be aged for a selected period of time. This is a very basic explanation of the winemaking process as there are numerous decisions and other steps that can be made during the production process. During a winery visit, ask the owner/ winemaker for a tour and an explanation of their process.

Three Major Types of Wine...

- Table wine: typically 8-15% alcohol
- Sparkling wine: typically 8-12% alcohol
- Fortified wine: typically 17-22% alcohol

Conversion Table...

| 1 acre = 2 to 10 tons of grapes | 1 ton of grapes = 2.33 barrels | 1 barrel = 25 cases | 1 case = 12 bottles | 1 bottle = 4-5 glasses |

White Wines Versus Red Wines...

It is the pigmentation of the grape skin and not the grape juice itself that determines the color of a wine. When white grapes are crushed, their skin is removed and the wine remains white. When red grapes (many have white insides) are crushed, their skin remains with the juice. Through absorption of the skin coloration, the wine becomes a purple-to-red color.

Common Grapes Grown in Colorado and their Wine Tastes and Characteristics...

Please note: This is a brief overview because grapes (and therefore the resultant wine) can have unique qualities all their own depending on terrior (see *Wine Terminology* section) and how the wines are produced.

WHITE

Chardonnay (shar-dun-nay):
- one of the most common white wines and is grown worldwide
- usually receives some "oak treatment" (via chips or barrel)
- an "unoaked" version ferments in stainless steel
- tastes from the oak: butterscotch / toasty / vanilla
- tastes from the grape: apple / pear / tropical fruit / subtle earthy

Gewürztraminer (geh-vertz-tra-mee-ner):
- can be sweet or dry
- tastes: lychee fruit / overripe peach or mango
- tastes: floral, although can be quite perfumed

Muscat (moos caht):
- possibly the oldest domesticated grape variety
- can be dry, but primarily used to make sweet dessert wine
- tastes: grapes / peach / rose petals

**Pinot Gris / Pinot Grigio
(pee-noh gree or pee-noh gree-jee-o):**
- becoming a rival to Chardonnay as the most asked-for white wine
- usually medium-bodied and low in acidity
- tastes: light apple or pear / some mineral / not oaky

Riesling (reese-ling):
- often thought of as a sweet German wine (not necessarily so)
- can be processed to be a sweet or dry wine
- often light-bodied, crisp and refreshing
- usually low to medium alcohol content
- tastes: fruity and flowery / some mineral

Sauvignon Blanc (saw-vee-nyon blahnk):
- distinctive, pungent flavors and aromas
- tastes: tart apple or pear / passion fruits / grapefruit
- tastes: crisp and tart / grassy and herbal

Sémillon (say-mee-yohn):
- usually used to blend with another grape
- tastes: citrus / apple / pear / ripe peach

Viognier (vee-own-yay):
- a tricky grape to grow and harvest
- medium-bodied with low acidity
- tastes: floral / apricot / mango / pineapple

RED

Barbera (bar-bear-rah):
- low tannin, but high acidity and often blended with other grapes
- tastes when young: cherry and raspberry
- tastes when aged: a crisp, big fruit wine

Cabernet Franc (cab-er-nay frahnk):

- a genetic parent to Cabernet Sauvignon and Sauvignon Blanc
- used alone or blended with other red wines
- lighter in tannin than Cabernet Sauvignon
- tastes: blackcurrant and raspberry / black licorice / vegetal

Cabernet Sauvignon (cab-er-nay saw-vee-nyon):

- one of the most common red wines and grows in most climates
- higher in tannin than other reds, although blending with another red grape can reduce the tannin impact
- medium- to full-bodied and softens with aging
- tastes: blackcurrants and other dark fruits
- tastes when aged: smoke / leather / chocolate / pepper

Grenache (greh-nosh):

- primarily blended with other wines or used in dessert wines
- a high-alcohol wine lacking tannin and color
- tastes: berry-flavored / allspice / cinnamon

Malbec (mall-beck):

- deeply colored, full-bodied and rich tannins
- tastes: plums / rich, red fruits / anise

Meritage (mar-it-tige):

- not a grape, but a term indicating 2 or more grapes (out of 8 permitted) were blended using the Bordeaux style of winemaking

Merlot (mer-low):
- used on its own or blended with Cabernet Sauvignon to reduce the level of tannin in the Cabernet
- low in tannin and usually full-bodied
- tastes: blackcurrants / plums / chocolate / earthy / spicy

Pinot Noir (pee-noh nwahr):
- can be a difficult grape to grow and harvest
- high alcohol with low to medium tannin
- tastes: like a blend of red fruits (cherry and raspberry) / spicy / herbal / earthy

Sangiovese (san-joe-vay-zay):
- can range from light- to full-bodied with medium tannin
- tastes: red fruits (strawberries to tart cherry) / sometimes a nutty or smoky taste

Syrah (sih-rah):
- in Australia is spelled Shiraz (sir-rahz)
- deeply colored, full-bodied with firm tannin
- tastes: dark fruit / pepper / licorice / tar

Tempranillo (temp-rah-nee-yoh):
- not often bottled as a stand-alone grape, but used as the base
- deep color, low acidity and high in tannin
- tastes: berries and plum / herbal / earthy / mineral

Zinfandel (zin-fan-dell):
- can be produced as a young, fruity wine or aged and complex

- can be used as a sweeter wine - White Zinfandel (not a grape)
- tastes: blackberry / black cherry / pepper / licorice

OTHER

Dessert Wines or Port:
- A higher alcohol content wine that is often fortified using additional alcohol. Very often these wines are quite sweet.

Fruit Wines:
- A fermented alcoholic beverage using fruit instead of grapes and is usually given the name from the fruit used.

Hard Cider:
- A fermented alcoholic beverage that is made from apple juice. Hard Cider can range from sweet to dry, and its appearance from cloudy to clear.

Ice Wine:
- A very sweet dessert wine whereby the grapes are frozen on the vine prior to fermentation to allow for a higher concentration of sugar.

Mead:
- An alcoholic beverage where the sugar comes from honey rather than grapes, can be sweet to dry.

WINE TERMINOLOGY

ACIDITY: A taste factor in white wines more than red. A high amount of acidity feels crisp, tart or sour, and low acidity feels soft or "flabby." Your mouth usually salivates with acidity. See Tannin.

AGING WINE: The length of time a wine remains in the bottle. Aging time depends on many factors, since some wines should be consumed "young" while others improve with age.

ALCOHOL CONTENT: Determined by the sugar level in the grape juice and to some extent the yeast during fermentation. See GRAPE VARIETIES section for more information.

AROMA, NOSE or BOUQUET: What your nose smells or perceives in the wine.

ASTRINGENT: An astringent wine will cause the mouth to pucker and is produced by the tannin in grape skins. Red wines have varying degrees of astringency.

AVA: Stands for American Viticultural Area, which is a designated geographic wine area having certain distinctive characteristics (see Terroir) for growing grapes. Colorado has two: Grand Valley and West Elks.

BALANCE: A combination of wine components (acidity, tannin, fruit, body and alcohol) and how well they work (or don't work) together.

BLIND TASTING: Where the taster knows nothing about the wine in the glass. DOUBLE-BLIND TASTING: Neither the taster nor the pourer know anything about the wine in the glass. Primarily used for competition.

BODY: How dense or thick the wine feels in your mouth. Wines are described as light-, medium- or full-bodied (water, milk, cream).

BREATHING or DECANTING: Pouring a bottle of wine into another container to allow it to "breathe" and mix with air.

BRIX: A measurement of sugar content in the grapes while on the vine. On average, grapes have 0% brix in June and +20% at harvest time.

COLOR: The tint or hue a wine has, this can vary from almost clear to deep golden for whites, and purple, ruby or brick for reds. See TASTING section for more information.

COMPLEXITY: A tasting term indicating a wine's ability to reveal (or not) additional flavors and characteristics on the palate after swallowing the wine.

CORKED: A term used to describe a tainted wine, which produces an off smell and/or taste; a bad bottle is said to be "corked".

CRISP: A term used to describe a sense or taste, referring to a tart, refreshing acidity in the wine.

CRUSH: A term used to describe the process of crushing grapes, usually done by a machine and not with your feet!

DENSITY: See Body.

DEPTH: A subjective measurement of how "dimensional" a wine is on your palate. See Complexity.

DRY WINE: A wine that has little or no sugar left after fermentation. The opposite would be SWEET WINE.

EARTHY: Various aromas or tastes that remind you of minerals, rocks, dry leaves or soil, can also include words such as musky, tobacco, leather, tar and burnt rubber.

ESTATE BOTTLED: A term indicating one company grew the grapes and made the wine.

FERMENTATION: A natural process that occurs when yeast comes in contact with sugar (in grapes or other fruit) and converts to alcohol.

FINISH: The impression a wine leaves in your mouth after you taste it. See Complexity.

FLIGHT: A sampling of several wines that can be organized by grape, region or vintage. This is what you normally experience at a Tasting Room. See Horizontal and Vertical Tasting.

FLORAL: A term given to aromas or tastes in wine suggesting flowers.

FORTIFIED WINE: Wine containing 17-22% alcohol and created by adding additional neutral alcohol; examples are dessert, port or sherry.

FRUITY: The aroma or taste of fruit in the wine; fruits include red, black, tropical, citrus or apple/pear. See TASTING section.

GRASSY and HERBAL: Aroma or taste terms that imply an earthy or plant characteristic, such as mint or hay.

HORIZONTAL TASTING: A sampling of similar wines from the same vintage but from different wineries. See Flight and Vertical Tasting.

LEGS: A term used in wine tasting when swirled wine gives the image of "legs" or "tears" on the inside of a glass.

LENGTH: How long the wine seems to remain on your palate after tasting. See Complexity.

MINERAL: A descriptive taste for wine, how a stone might taste in your mouth.

NEW WORLD WINES: Wines that come from anywhere but Europe.

OAK BARREL: Used for storing wine as it matures and ages prior to bottling. An oak barrel can have a profound impact on the taste of the wine depending on where the oak tree originates, how the barrel is made and the number of uses. In the United States, barrels are usually described as either American or French, although that does not indicate tree origin.

OAKY: A term given to white wines (particularly Chardonnay) to indicate an aroma and/or taste of oak. Many wineries use oak chips and/or barrels to create this taste during the fermentation process.

OLD WORLD WINES: Wines that come from Europe.

OENOLOGY (ee-nol-o-gee): The science and study of wine and winemaking. An OENOLOGIST is an expert in the field. See Viticulture.

OXIDIZED: A term used to describe a flaw in wine that has been exposed to too much oxygen.

PUNGENT: An aroma or taste used to describe a wine's flavor.

RESERVE WINES: A term used by New World Wines (or Old World selling to New World) to indicate something "special" about the wine; it is not a regulated term and therefore not considered particularly meaningful.

SOMMELIER (some-all-yeah): A trained and knowledgeable wine professional who has completed several courses of study.

SPICY or PEPPERY: Tastes on your palate that remind you of various spices, such as cinnamon, pepper or cloves.

STAINLESS STEEL TANK: Used for storing wine as it matures and ages prior to bottling; sometimes used as a temporary storage prior to aging the wine in an oak barrel (see Oak Barrel). Stainless steel tanks offer a winemaker a "neutral" container.

SULFITES: Used as a preservative in wine to maintain freshness and prevent oxidation, also occurs naturally during fermentation.

SWEETNESS: One of the four taste perceptions on the tongue besides SOUR, BITTER and SALTY.

TANNIN: A by-product of the seeds, stems and grapes used in red winemaking. Tannin can be a soft, velvety sensation to a bitter, overpowering feeling. Your mouth usually puckers from tannin. See Astringent and Acidity.

TERROIR (tare-wahr): A French term that cannot be exactly translated, but refers to the natural effects of land, soil, climate, growing season and conditions in a particular area.

TYPICITY: How true the wine is to the "standard" taste for that grape variety.

UNOAKED: Wines that have not received any oak treatment.

VERTICAL TASTING: A sampling of wines (usually the same type) all from the same producer, but from different vintages. See Horizontal Tasting.

VINIFICATION: The production of taking grapes and making them into wine.

VINTAGE: The year on a wine bottle referencing the year the grapes were harvested.

VITICULTURE: The process of growing grapes.

VITIS VINIFERA: The primary grape species used for winemaking.

WINE AROMA WHEEL: A device which provides words to help explain smells and flavors in wine, beginning with general terms and branching out to more specific words. (See WineAromaWheel.com.)

WINE CLUB: A feature offered by wineries providing discounts and specials on their wines.

YEAST: A naturally occurring one-celled organism that is present on grape skins. See Fermentation.

YOUNG: A wine that is meant to be drunk with little aging.

YUCK: My word used to describe a wine that tastes terrible!

Grand Valley Region

Wine Fact

Cork was developed as a
bottle closure in the late
seventeenth-century.
It was only after this that bottles
were lain down for aging,
and the bottle shapes
slowly changed from
short and bulbous
to tall and slender.

http://www.beekmanwine.com/factsquotes.htm

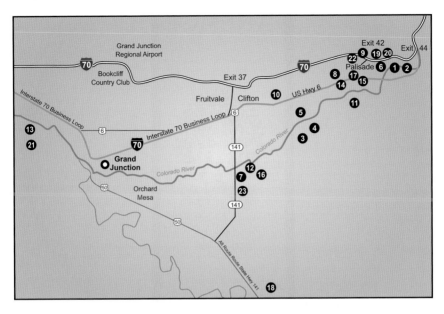

Grand Valley Region Wineries

1. Anemoi Wines
2. Canyon Wind Cellars
3. Carlson Vineyards
4. Colorado Cellars Winery
5. Colterris Wines
6. DeBeque Canyon Winery
7. Desert Sun Vineyards
8. Garfield Estates Vineyard & Winery
9. Grande River Vineyards
10. Graystone Winery
11. Gubbini Winery
12. Hermosa Vineyards

13. Kahil Winery
14. Maison la Belle Vie
15. Meadery of the Rockies
16. Mesa Park Vineyards
17. Plum Creek Cellars
18. Reeder Mesa Vineyards
19. St. Kathryn Cellars
20. Talon Winery
21. Two Rivers Winery
22. Varaison Vineyards & Winery
23. Whitewater Hill Vineyards

ANEMOI WINES

3907 N. River Road, Palisade, CO 81526
970-464-0888
anemoiwines.com
info@anemoiwines.com

OWNER: Jay & Jennifer Christianson

YEAR BEGAN OPERATION: 2011

AVERAGE CASES PRODUCED ANNUALLY: 2,000

WINES PRODUCED:
White: None
Red: None
Other: Blends called Boreas, Zephyrus, Notus, Eurus, Lapyx

MESSAGE FROM OWNER: Jay and Jennifer Christianson, owners/
winemakers of Canyon Wind Cellars, created Anemoi Wines as a result
of their love of big, fruit-forward, oaky New World wines, and the
realization that no such wine was currently produced in Colorado.

The Anemoi were the mythological Greek Gods of wind, named for
the cardinal direction from which their winds came. The primary gods
were Boreas (North Wind), Eurus (East Wind), Notus (South Wind)
and Zephyrus (West Wind). The Anemoi are still very much alive and
play a key role in the creation of our wines. Like the personalities of
the winds, each wine possesses distinctive characteristics produced by
the winds and ever-changing weather. Each Anemoi wine is named for
the god that best represents its individuality and reflects its growing
season. It was the cool summer of 2009 that led to the creation of our
first wine, Boreas, and the genesis of Anemoi Wines.

TASTING ROOM INFORMATION: Daily, from 10 a.m. to 5 p.m.

DIRECTIONS: From I-70 westbound at Exit #44: Turn slightly right
(southwest) onto N. River Road; winery is .5 miles ahead on left.

From I-70 eastbound at Exit #42: Turn right (south) onto Elberta
Avenue (37 3/10 Road); turn left (east) onto W. 1st Street / G 4/10 Road;
turn right (south) onto Main Street; turn left (east) onto E. 3rd Street,
which turns into N. River Road. Winery is 1.5 miles down River Road
on right.

OTHER AMENITIES AT WINERY: A boutique tasting room with
gourmet foods, wine accessories, kitchen goods and home décor;
outdoor picnic and wedding facilities and underground barrel cellar.

WINE AVAILABLE FOR PURCHASE OUTSIDE OF WINERY: Yes

OTHER TASTING ROOM LOCATIONS: Canyon Wind Cellars Tasting
Room (see Mountain Region)

NOTES: _____

_____

_____

_____

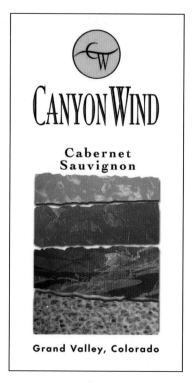

CANYON WIND CELLARS

3907 N. River Road, Palisade, CO 81526
970-464-0888
canyonwindcellars.com
info@canyonwindcellars.com

OWNER: Jay & Jennifer Christianson

YEAR BEGAN OPERATION: 1996

AVERAGE CASES PRODUCED ANNUALLY: 5,000

WINES PRODUCED:
White: Chardonnay, Pinot Grigio, Sauvignon Blanc
Red: Cabernet Franc, Cabernet Sauvignon, Merlot, Petit Verdot, Syrah
Other: Blends called 47-Ten Red, 47-Ten Rosé, 47-Ten White Blend, Port wine, IV

MESSAGE FROM OWNER: Founded in 1996, Canyon Wind Cellars is a family-owned, estate winery named for the mountain breezes that keep the fruit on our vineyard cool under the hot, Colorado sun. With the assistance of renowned Napa Winemaker, Robert Pepi, the Christianson family produces award-winning, signature wines utilizing low-intervention winemaking and sustainable practices.

TASTING ROOM INFORMATION: Daily, from 10 a.m. to 5 p.m.

DIRECTIONS: From I-70 westbound at Exit #44: Turn slightly right (southwest) onto N. River Road; winery is .5 miles ahead on left.

From I-70 eastbound at Exit #42: Turn right (south) onto Elberta Avenue (37 3/10 Road); turn left (east) onto W. 1st Street / G 4/10 Road; turn right (south) onto Main Street; turn left (east) onto E. 3rd Street, which turns into N. River Road. Winery is 1.5 miles down River Road on right.

OTHER AMENITIES AT WINERY: A boutique tasting room with gourmet foods, wine accessories, kitchen goods and home décor; outdoor picnic and wedding facilities and underground barrel cellar.

WINE AVAILABLE FOR PURCHASE OUTSIDE OF WINERY: Yes

OTHER TASTING ROOM LOCATIONS: Canyon Wind Cellars Tasting Room (see Mountain Region)

NOTES: _____

_____

_____

_____

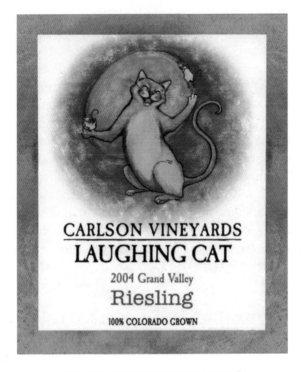

CARLSON VINEYARDS

461 35 Road, Palisade, CO 81526
970-464-5554
carlsonvineyards.com
info@carlsonvineyards.com

OWNER: Parker and Mary Carlson

YEAR BEGAN OPERATION: 1998

AVERAGE CASES PRODUCED ANNUALLY: 10,000

WINES PRODUCED:
White: Chardonnay, Gewürztraminer, Riesling
Red: Lemberger, Merlot, Shiraz
Others: Blends called Laughing Cat Sweet Baby Red and Prairie Dog
Blush, Fruit wines, Dessert wines

MESSAGE FROM OWNER: At Carlson Vineyards, wine is not treated as the nectar of snobs! One step into the winery will show you that the Carlsons put their hearts, skill and wit into making superb wines that you will enjoy. Situated in a semi-arid landscape, this protected, high-altitude valley cut by the Colorado River produces remarkable wines. Sinfully flavorful wine grapes and fruits flourish under the care of neighboring growers. Carlson wines are known for capturing these pure, Colorado-grown fruit aromas and flavors.

In the tasting room, Parker Carlson and staff are on hand to pour samples and to chat. Notice all the medals dangling from wine bottles lining the walls. Just ask, and they will take you back into the winery to show you the winemaking process. They will also give you advice, tips and recipes on what to have with Carlson wines, and most certainly, turn you into a believer that wine is a fun adventure!

TASTING ROOM INFORMATION: Daily, from 10 a.m. to 5:45 p.m.

DIRECTIONS: From I-70 westbound at Exit #44: Exit becomes Hwy 6 (G Road); turn left (south) onto 38 Road; follow main road; turn left (south) onto 36 Road; turn right (west) onto E. 1/2 Road; turn left (south) onto 35 1/2 Road; turn right (west) onto E Road; turn left (south) onto 35 Road.

From I-70 eastbound at Exit #37: Follow I-70 Business (32 Road) south; turn left (east) onto C 1/2 Road; turn left (north) onto 34 1/2 Road; turn right (east) onto D Road, which changes to 35 Road.

OTHER AMENITIES AT WINERY: A gift shop and picnic area

WINE AVAILABLE FOR PURCHASE OUTSIDE OF WINERY: Yes

OTHER TASTING ROOM LOCATIONS: No

NOTES: _____

_____

_____

_____

COLORADO CELLARS WINERY

3553 E Road, Palisade, CO 81526
970-464-7921 or 800-848-2812
coloradocellars.com
info@coloradocellars.com

OWNER: Richard and Padte Turley

YEAR BEGAN OPERATION: 1978

AVERAGE CASES PRODUCED ANNUALLY: 20,000 - 25,000

WINES PRODUCED:
White: Chardonnay, Gewürztraminer, Pinot Grigio, White Riesling
Red: Cabernet Sauvignon, Merlot, Syrah
Other: Blends called Eclipse Sweet Red, Colorado Mountain
Vineyards Red Table Wine, Road Kill Red; Alpenrosé, Champagne,
numerous Fruit wines, Port wines and Meads.

MESSAGE FROM OWNER: Colorado Cellars Winery is Colorado's oldest, largest and most award-winning winery. Founded in 1978 as Colorado Mountain Vineyards, today's brands also include Rocky Mountain Vineyards and the Orchard Mesa Wine Company. Colorado Cellars is a family-owned and operated winery, so winemaking here is truly a way of life. We grow our own grapes and fruit, keep bees for honey wine, personally make and bottle our wines and even deliver it ourselves! We are unique amongst Colorado wineries in that we are (and always have been) exclusively in the wine business. Today we continue to sell wines made under old Colorado Winery License #5, the state's oldest license still in existence!

TASTING ROOM INFORMATION: Summer, Monday through Friday from 9 a.m. to 5 p.m., Saturday from 10 a.m. to 5 p.m. Winter, Monday through Friday from 9 a.m. to 4 p.m., Saturday from 11 a.m. to 5 p.m. Closed Sundays.

DIRECTIONS: From I-70 westbound at Exit #44: Exit becomes Hwy 6 (G Road); turn left (south) onto 38 Road; follow main road; turn left (south) onto 36 Road; turn right (west) onto E. 1/2 Road; turn left (south) onto 35 1/2 Road; turn left (east) onto E Road.

From I-70 eastbound at Exit #37: Follow I-70 Business (32 Road) south; turn left (east) onto C 1/2 Road; turn left (north) onto 34 1/2 Road; turn right (east) onto D Road, which changes to 35 Road; turn right (east) onto E Road.

OTHER AMENITIES AT WINERY: Food, dessert and cooking products made with wine as well as facilities for meetings and weddings.

WINE AVAILABLE FOR PURCHASE OUTSIDE OF WINERY: Yes

OTHER TASTING ROOM LOCATIONS: No

NOTES: _____

_____

_____

_____

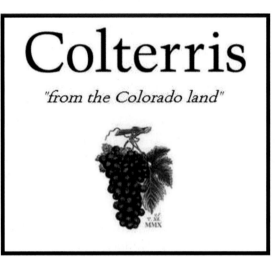

COLTERRIS WINES

3548 E 1/2 Road, Palisade, CO 81526

Mailing address: PO Box 1405, Palisade, CO 81526

970-464-1150

colterris.com

theresa@colterris.com

OWNER: Theresa High

YEAR BEGAN OPERATION: 2011

AVERAGE CASES PRODUCED ANNUALLY: 2,500

WINES PRODUCED:
White: None
Red: Cabernet Franc, Cabernet Sauvignon
Other: None

MESSAGE FROM OWNER: Colterris Wines began operations in January 2010 and its name was derived by combining a three-letter abbreviation of Colorado "Col" with the Latin word "terris" meaning from the land. Our Cabernet Sauvignon originates primarily from grapes grown in the sun and soil of Theresa's Vineyard on East Orchard Mesa, located in Colorado's beautiful and picturesque Western Slope. Situated in the heart of the Grand Valley AVA, this unique vineyard site at 4,600' is protected by the foothills of the Grand Mesa and by close proximity to the Colorado River. This combination of high altitude sunlight and cool river nights produce a distinctively bold, red wine, rich in color, flavor and smooth tannins. I am extremely encouraged about the future potential of wines being produced here.

TASTING ROOM INFORMATION: July through September, daily, from 10 a.m. to 5 p.m. Off-season by appointment only.

DIRECTIONS: From I-70 westbound at Exit #44: Exit becomes Hwy 6 (G Road); turn left (south) onto 38 Road; follow main road; turn left (south) onto 36 Road; turn right (west) onto E 1/2 Road. We are at the junction of E 1/2 Road and 35 1/2 Road.
   From I-70 eastbound at Exit #37: Follow I-70 Business (32 Road) south; turn left (east) onto C 1/2 Road; turn left (north) onto 34 1/2 Road; turn right (east) onto D Road, which changes to 35 Road; turn right (east) onto E Road; turn left (north) onto 35 1/2 Road. We are at the junction of E 1/2 Road and 35 1/2 Road.

OTHER AMENITIES AT WINERY: We provide "agritours" of the orchards, vineyards and gardens. We host weddings, feasts in the field and corporate events at our outside pavilion with 360 degree views. We have a Country Store where guests can purchase fruit, fruit products and gift items.

WINE AVAILABLE FOR PURCHASE OUTSIDE OF WINERY: Yes

OTHER TASTING ROOM LOCATIONS: No

NOTES: _____

_____

_____

_____

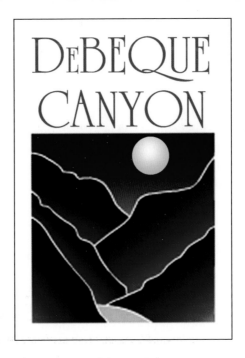

DEBEQUE CANYON WINERY

144 Kluge Street, Bldg. 3, Palisade CO 81526
Mailing address: PO Box 1391, Palisade CO 81526
970-464-0550
debequecanyonwinery.com
debequecanyonwines@bresnan.net

OWNER: Bennett and Davelyn (Davy) Price

YEAR BEGAN OPERATION: 1997

AVERAGE CASES PRODUCED ANNUALLY: 3,500

WINES PRODUCED:
White: Chardonnay, Gewürztraminer, Riesling, Viognier
Red: Cabernet Franc, Cabernet Sauvignon, Malbec, Merlot,
Syrah, Tempranillo
Other: Blend called Claret, Port wines

MESSAGE FROM OWNER: Early pioneers in the Colorado wine industry, Bennett and Davy Price designed and planted vineyards for most of the wineries in the Grand Valley. Bennett was a home-winemaker, who studied at the University of California at Davis, established friendships with a number of California winemakers and refined his winemaking style. They are best known for red wines which are full-bodied and well-aged in French oak.

Their white wines are especially noted for their fruit-forward flavors and smooth, yet slightly dry finish. As a special interest, they have crafted many Port-style wines that have won numerous awards. Recently, their daughter and grandson have joined their endeavors, making this a true, family winery.

TASTING ROOM INFORMATION: May through September, daily, from 10 a.m. to 6 p.m.; October through April, Sunday through Friday from noon to 5 p.m., Saturday from 10 a.m. to 5 p.m. Also available by appointment.

DIRECTIONS: From I-70 at Exit #42: Head south on Elberta Avenue (37 3/10 Road); turn left (east) onto 1st Street; turn right (south) onto Kluge Street; turn right (west) onto 2nd Street (just before RR tracks) to Building #3 on the right.

OTHER AMENITIES AT WINERY: Wine-related gifts. The tasting room, located inside the Winery, is available for special barrel tastings.

WINE AVAILABLE FOR PURCHASE OUTSIDE OF WINERY: Yes

OTHER TASTING ROOM LOCATIONS: Coyote Creek Arts Studio/Gallery (see Pikes Peak Region)

NOTES: _____

_____

_____

_____

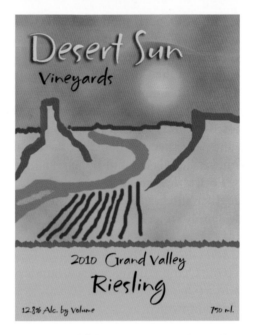

DESERT SUN VINEYARDS

3230 B 1/2 Road, Grand Junction, CO 81503
970-434-9851
desertsunvineyards.com
doug@desertsunvineyards.com

OWNER: Doug and Kathryn Hovde

YEAR BEGAN OPERATION: 2008

AVERAGE CASES PRODUCED ANNUALLY: 50

WINES PRODUCED:
White: Chardonnay, Riesling
Red: Cabernet Sauvignon, Zinfandel
Other: None

MESSAGE FROM OWNER: Desert Sun Vineyards is a small, family-owned vineyard and winery. We take advantage of the wonderful terroir that the Grand Valley has, and make high quality wines. Please come and enjoy!

TASTING ROOM INFORMATION: May through November, Friday through Sunday from 11 a.m. to 5 p.m.

DIRECTIONS: From the intersection of I-70 and Exit #37: Head south on I-70 Business (Hwy 141); turn left (south) onto 32 Road; turn left (east) onto B 1/2 Road.

OTHER AMENITIES AT WINERY: N/A

WINE AVAILABLE FOR PURCHASE OUTSIDE OF WINERY: Yes

OTHER TASTING ROOM LOCATIONS: No

NOTES: _____

_____

_____

_____

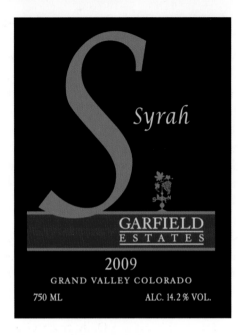

GARFIELD ESTATES VINEYARD AND WINERY

3572 G Road, Palisade, CO 81526
970-464-0941
garfieldestates.com
info@garfieldestates.com

OWNER: Jeff and Carol Carr, Founders; Mike McNamara, Business Partner

YEAR BEGAN OPERATION: 2000

AVERAGE CASES PRODUCED ANNUALLY: 3,000

WINES PRODUCED:
White: Fumé Blanc, Viognier
Red: Cabernet Franc, Syrah
Other: Blend called S2; Vin de Glace (Ice wine);
Vin au Chocolat (Port wine)

MESSAGE FROM OWNER: Since planting our first estate vineyards in early 2000, Garfield Estates Vineyard and Winery has been committed to a simple and focused philosophy: "Produce world-class wines using 100% Colorado Estate grown grapes that are food- and consumer-friendly." This means sustainable practices in the vineyard and competitive prices for our wines.

Making a great wine requires three things: the best grapes, state-of-the-art equipment and a highly skilled winemaker—at Garfield Estates we have invested in all three. We carefully grow and manage our own vineyards because we want the highest quality grapes available to craft our wines. No over-cropped, bulk wine grapes for our wines; we don't just grow grapes—we grow wine.

Our highly skilled winemaker has crafted wines in Europe and the United States, and our facility incorporates state-of-the-art equipment that would compare to any wineries in Napa. We are very passionate about our wines, and set the bar higher with each wine, year after year.

TASTING ROOM INFORMATION: Daily, from 11 a.m. to 5 p.m.

DIRECTIONS: From the intersection of I-70 and Exit #42 in Palisade: Head south on Elberta Avenue (37 3/10 Road); turn right (west) onto G Road/Hwy 6; at approximately 1/2 mile, turn right (west) onto G Road. The winery is on the right (north) side of G Road.

OTHER AMENITIES AT WINERY: Vineyard tours available upon request

WINE AVAILABLE FOR PURCHASE OUTSIDE OF WINERY: Yes

OTHER TASTING ROOM LOCATIONS: Colorado Winery Row (see Front Range Region)

NOTES: _____

_____

_____

_____

GRANDE RIVER VINEYARDS

787 N. Elberta Avenue, Palisade, CO 81526
Mailing address: PO Box 129, Palisade, CO 81526
970-464-5867 or 800-264-7696
granderiverwines.com
info@granderiverwines.com

OWNER: Stephen and Naomi Smith

YEAR BEGAN OPERATION: 1990

AVERAGE CASES PRODUCED ANNUALLY: 5,000

WINES PRODUCED:
White: Chardonnay, Sauvignon Blanc, Viognier
Red: Cabernet Franc, Cabernet Sauvignon, Malbec, Merlot, Syrah
Other: Blends called Meritage White and Meritage Red, Semi-Sweet, Sweet Red, Desert Blush, Port wine and Late Harvest Viognier (dessert wines)

MESSAGE FROM OWNER: Grande River Vineyards started planting grapes in 1987, when there were only three wineries in Colorado, and produced our first vintage in 1990, becoming Colorado's fifth winery. We were Colorado's largest grape grower until selling much of our farming operation to local fruit growers in 2006, although we continue to farm about ten acres of grapes.

We make wines from the classic European wine varieties in traditional styles. Our wines have won hundreds of awards in regional, national and international competitions. We consider ourselves to be the Gateway to Colorado's Wine Country, a good place to start your wine country tour! We are a Premium Winegrowing Estate as many of our wines are estate grown, produced and bottled, and all wines are made from Colorado-grown grapes. We are also Colorado's Solar Powered Winery.

Come visit our old-world-style tasting room and try some of our delicious wines, stroll through our demonstration vineyard and taste the different varieties of grapes, join us for a concert, host an event or join our wine club. You can also visit us online where you can place orders for shipment to over 20 states.

TASTING ROOM INFORMATION: Daily, from 9:00 a.m. to 5:00 p.m.

DIRECTIONS: From I-70 at Exit #42: Head south on Elberta Avenue (37 3/10 Road); turn right (west) at Grande River Drive; we are on the left under the large sign.

OTHER AMENITIES AT WINERY: We have facilities for small group meetings, catered dinners (no restaurant but two kitchens) in our cellar and an outdoor venue for concerts or weddings.

WINE AVAILABLE FOR PURCHASE OUTSIDE OF WINERY: Yes

OTHER TASTING ROOM LOCATIONS: No

NOTES: _____

_____

_____

_____

GRAYSTONE WINERY

3352 F Road, Clifton, CO 81520
970-434-8610
graystonewine.com
graystone@acsol.net

OWNER: Barb Maurer

YEAR BEGAN OPERATION: 2001

AVERAGE CASES PRODUCED ANNUALLY: 1,000 - 2,000

WINES PRODUCED:
White: None
Red: None
Other: Port wines

MESSAGE FROM OWNER: Founded in 2001, this small, boutique-style winery specializes in Port wines. It is named for the gray, majestic, shale bluffs surrounding the Grand Valley and Colorado River.

It is under the direction of owner and winemaker, Barb Maurer's meticulous hand and personal tastes, that Graystone Winery's three exquisite ports are created. Winemaking wasn't always her chosen career path. However, armed with an MBA from Methodist University and a JD from Gonzaga University, Barb enrolled in an online wine-making class from University of California at Davis. Shortly thereafter, she met California winemaking consultant, Richard Bruno, who taught her how to make Port. Come in and sample our three delicious varieties!

TASTING ROOM INFORMATION: May through October, Monday through Saturday from 10 a.m. to 6 p.m., Sunday from 11 a.m. to 6p.m.; November through April, Monday through Saturday from 10 a.m. to 5 p.m., Sunday from 11 a.m. to 5 p.m.

DIRECTIONS: From I-70 and Exit #37 near Grand Junction: Head south on Business Hwy 70; turn left (east) onto Hwy 6 (F Road); stay on Hwy 6 past 33 3/8 Road; just after 33 3/8 Road, turn right (east) onto F Road, where Hwy 6 and F Road separate.

OTHER AMENITIES AT WINERY: Gift shop; venue for small events

WINE AVAILABLE FOR PURCHASE OUTSIDE OF WINERY: Yes

OTHER TASTING ROOM LOCATIONS: No

NOTES: _____

_____

_____

_____

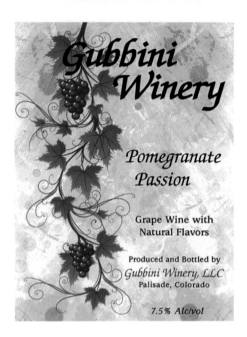

GUBBINI WINERY
3697 F Road, Palisade, CO 81526
970-464-5608 or 970-270-7185
Website: N/A
GubbiniWinery@aol.com

OWNER: Linda Lee Gubbini

YEAR BEGAN OPERATION: 2008

AVERAGE CASES PRODUCED ANNUALLY: Information not Available

WINES PRODUCED:
White: Gewürztraminer, Riesling
Red: Various Italian reds, Pinot Noir
Other: Dessert wines

MESSAGE FROM OWNER: It all started in 1990 with the purchase of a stone fruit orchard and homestead that was re-cultivated in 1999 into what is now Horse Mountain Vineyards. After extensive research of grape varietals, Syrah and Riesling were selected as the most compatible for the Palisade region and climate. After many seasons of learning the subtleties of grape cultivation, the yields improved and became recognized for their high quality. Presently, the grapes are being purchased and made into award-winning wines by prominent Front Range winemakers.

Being full-blooded Italian, Linda Lee Gubbini had the passion to begin producing wines under her own unique label. In 2011, Gubbini Winery opened its doors and welcomed its first guests to a home-style tasting room, which makes one feel as though they just stopped by a friend's house for a glass of wine. Gubbini Winery is able to offer a wide range of wines, and future plans include producing its own estate wines from Horse Mountain Vineyard grapes. Growing grapes and producing wine is an adventure and labor of love. Gubbini Winery welcomes all to enjoy the wine and hospitality in its tasting room in Palisade.

TASTING ROOM INFORMATION: April through December, Friday through Sunday from 11 a.m. to 6 p.m.; other times by appointment.

DIRECTIONS: From the intersection of I-70 and Exit #42 in Palisade: Head south on Elberta Avenue (37 3/10 Road); turn left (east) onto W. 8th Street/Hwy 6; turn right (south) onto 38 Road, which changes to F 1/2 Road; turn left (south) onto 37 1/4 Road; turn right (west) onto F Road.

OTHER AMENITIES AT WINERY: Wine-related merchandise; self-guided vineyard tour.

WINE AVAILABLE FOR PURCHASE OUTSIDE OF WINERY: No

OTHER TASTING ROOM LOCATIONS: No

NOTES: _____

_____

_____

_____

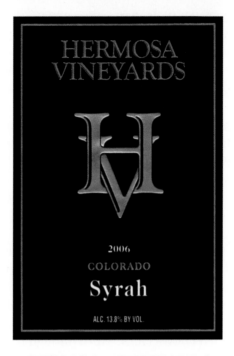

HERMOSA VINEYARDS
3269 3/4 C Road, Palisade, CO 81526
970-640-0940
hermosavineyards.com
hermosavineyards@aol.com

OWNER: Kenn Dunn

YEAR BEGAN OPERATION: 2001

AVERAGE CASES PRODUCED ANNUALLY: Information not Available

WINES PRODUCED:
White: Chardonnay, Gewürztraminer, Riesling, Viognier
Red: Cabernet Franc, Cabernet Sauvignon, Merlot, Syrah
Other: Dessert wine

MESSAGE FROM OWNER: In 2001, after years of growing premium grapes for other wineries in Colorado, Kenn Dunn founded Hermosa Vineyards, LLC, a Limited Colorado Winery. Located in the Grand Valley, the winery is dedicated to handcrafting the finest wine from grapes grown in the high mountain desert of western Colorado. All of our wines are produced in very limited quantities. Our goal is not to be one of the biggest wineries, but one of the very best. With some excellent wineries located in Colorado, who are producing premium wines, we are in good company!

TASTING ROOM INFORMATION: Daily, usually from 11 a.m. to 5 p.m. or by appointment.

DIRECTIONS: From I-70 and Exit #37: Head south on I-70 Business (32 Road); turn left (east) onto C Road; at 3269 C Road, follow winery signs.

OTHER AMENITIES AT WINERY: Picnic tables

WINE AVAILABLE FOR PURCHASE OUTSIDE OF WINERY: Yes

OTHER TASTING ROOM LOCATIONS: No

NOTES: _____

_____

_____

_____

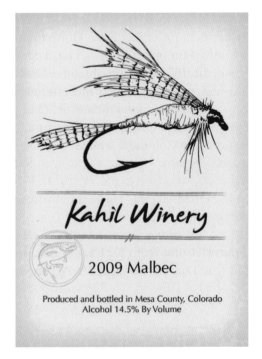

KAHIL WINERY
2087 Broadway, Grand Junction, CO 81507
970-640-3541
Website: coming soon
KahilWinery@hotmail.com

OWNER: Tyrel and Kathryn Lawson

YEAR BEGAN OPERATION: 2010

AVERAGE CASES PRODUCED ANNUALLY: 1,000

WINES PRODUCED:
(Adding other varietals over the next few years)
White: Pinot Gris
Red: Malbec
Other: None

MESSAGE FROM OWNER: Owner and winemaker, Tyrel Lawson is a Grand Valley native. Possessing a background in farming and ranching, he began working in the vineyard at Two Rivers Winery in 2004 and took over as winemaker in 2008. The initial setup of Kahil Winery began in 2009, as its first wine - a Malbec - was produced. Currently, Kahil Winery has four acres planted, which are divided between Malbec, Pinot Gris and Pinot Noir, in Eckert, Colorado. Another two acres of Malbec will be planted in 2012 in the Grand Valley.

The Malbec is a full-bodied red wine, that is fruit forward and approachable, and has the structure to pair well with food, but can be enjoyed on its own. The Pinot Gris is produced in a slightly non-traditional style, leaving a slight residual sugar and maintaining quite a bit of citrus, peach and tropical fruit on both the nose and palate. It is a great wine for everything, from the backyard summer BBQ to complementing the Thanksgiving turkey. Kahil Winery strives to produce small batch, high quality wines, that will hopefully showcase that there are good wines being produced in Colorado!

TASTING ROOM INFORMATION: By appointment only

DIRECTIONS: From the intersection of I-70 and Exit #28 (Redlands Parkway): Head south on Redlands Parkway; turn right (northwest) onto Broadway/Hwy 340. The winery is 2 miles up the road on left. (Note: GPS users should use Hwy 340 rather than Broadway.)

OTHER AMENITIES AT WINERY: N/A

WINE AVAILABLE FOR PURCHASE OUTSIDE OF WINERY: Yes

OTHER TASTING ROOM LOCATIONS: No

NOTES: _____

_____

_____

_____

MAISON LA BELLE VIE WINERY
3575 G Road, Palisade, CO 81526
970-464-4959
maisonlabellevie.com
frenchybar@aol.com

OWNER: John Barbier and Garry Wright

YEAR BEGAN OPERATION: 2004

AVERAGE CASES PRODUCED ANNUALLY: 1,000

WINES PRODUCED:
White: None
Red: Cabernet Sauvignon, Merlot, Syrah
Other: Bordeaux-style reds and blends, Dessert wine, Walnut Port,
Vin de Peche (Ice wine)

MESSAGE FROM OWNER: My name is John Barbier, and I am French. I have been in the food and wine industry for over 25 years. My family has been in the industry for many generations, in the Loire Valley in France.

In addition to being a winemaker, I am a chef and love to cook and show my customers that we have much to offer in Palisade, Colorado. Our wines are very authentic and we even use a recipe handed down through several generations.

We "dry farm" and do not use any chemicals in the vineyards. We are still stomping grapes with our feet and do everything by hand. We use only French oak to age our wines. Our venue is very welcoming, so please come and enjoy a unique experience at Maison la Belle Vie, which means "house of the beautiful life."

TASTING ROOM INFORMATION: Summer, daily, from 11 a.m. to 6 p.m.; Other times by appointment only.

DIRECTIONS: From the intersection of I-70 at Exit #42: Head south on Elberta Avenue (37 3/10 Road); turn right (west) onto G Road; stay straight on G Road past 36 Road.

OTHER AMENITIES AT WINERY: Outdoor patio and dining under the willows; wine dinners, weddings and other events at Amy's Courtyard.

WINE AVAILABLE FOR PURCHASE OUTSIDE OF WINERY: Yes

OTHER TASTING ROOM LOCATIONS: No

NOTES: _____

_____

_____

_____

MEADERY OF THE ROCKIES

3701 G Road, Palisade, CO 81526
970-464-7899
meaderyoftherockies.com
Michael@talonwinebrands.com

OWNER: Glenn and Natalie Foster

YEAR BEGAN OPERATION: 1996

AVERAGE CASES PRODUCED ANNUALLY: 10,000 (for all 3 labels)

WINES PRODUCED:
White: None
Red: None
Other: Meads called King Arthur, Lancelot, Guinevere, Camelot, Apricots 'n Honey, Peaches 'n Honey, Strawberries 'n Honey, Cherrie's 'n Honey, Raspberries 'n Honey, Blackberries 'n Honey, Raspberry Chocolate Satin, Blackberry Satin, Chocolate Cherry Satin, and Honey Shere'

MESSAGE FROM OWNER: Meadery of the Rockies is owned by Glenn and Natalie Foster, who have been involved in commercial wineries in the Grand Valley since 1995. Having founded Talon Winery in 2005, the Fosters acquired Meadery of the Rockies and St. Kathryn Cellars in 2008 in order to increase their production capacity. All wines are produced at the Meadery of the Rockies.

    If you can call ahead to arrange a time, tours of the winery are available, where you will learn all about their production methods. Meadery of the Rockies offers about 15 different meads, including traditionals, melomels and fortified dessert meads.

TASTING ROOM INFORMATION: Daily, from 10:00 a.m. to 5:00 p.m.

DIRECTIONS: From I-70 and Exit #42: Head south on Elberta Avenue (37 3/10 Road); turn right (west) onto G Road. The Meadery of the Rockies will be ¼ mile down on your right.

OTHER AMENITIES AT WINERY: We have a wonderful gift shop selling honey-related items and wine paraphernalia.

WINE AVAILABLE FOR PURCHASE OUTSIDE OF WINERY: Yes

OTHER TASTING ROOM LOCATIONS: Talon Winery and St. Kathryn Cellars (see Grand Valley Region); Honeyville Tasting Room (see Four Corners Region)

NOTES: _____

_____

_____

_____

MESA PARK VINEYARDS
3321 C Road, Palisade, CO 81526
970-434-4191
mesaparkvineyards.com
pricebooker@aol.com

OWNER: Brooke and Brad Webb, Patty and Chuck Price

YEAR BEGAN OPERATION: 2009

AVERAGE CASES PRODUCED ANNUALLY: 750

WINES PRODUCED:
White: Riesling (coming soon)
Red: Cabernet Franc, Cabernet Sauvignon, Merlot
Other: Family Reserve Red; Rosé and Port wine (coming soon)

MESSAGE FROM OWNER: Our family handcrafts premium, estate-grown red wines. Visit our estate - a beautiful vineyard of the classics: Merlot, Cabernet Sauvignon and Cabernet Franc.

TASTING ROOM INFORMATION: April through November, Thursday through Monday from 11 a.m. to 5:00 p.m.; December through March by appointment only.

DIRECTIONS: From I-70 and Exit #37: Head south on Elberta Avenue (37 3/10 Road); turn left (south) onto 32 Road; turn left (east) onto C Road.

OTHER AMENITIES AT WINERY: We can accommodate small groups of up to 35 people and have ample space for picnics.

WINE AVAILABLE FOR PURCHASE OUTSIDE OF WINERY: Yes

OTHER TASTING ROOM LOCATIONS: No

NOTES: _____

_____

_____

_____

PLUM CREEK CELLARS
3708 G Road, Palisade, CO 81526
970-464-7586
plumcreekwinery.com
plumcreekwinery@att.net

OWNER: Sue Phillips

YEAR BEGAN OPERATION: 1984

AVERAGE CASES PRODUCED ANNUALLY: Information not Available

WINES PRODUCED:
White: Chardonnay, Riesling, Sauvignon Blanc
Red: Cabernet Franc, Cabernet Sauvignon, Merlot, Sangiovese, Syrah
Other: Blends called Palisade Red, Palisade Festival, Palisade Rosé,
Grand Mesa Meritage, Dessert wines

MESSAGE FROM OWNER: Plum Creek Winery offers an authentic sense of Colorado terroir. Sourcing grapes from local vineyards has been our touchstone, since Doug and Sue Phillips founded the winery in 1984. Plum Creek has held true to this commitment of making Colorado-grown wines for more than 28 vintages, all the while maintaining a standard of excellence and consistency.

In addition to using grapes from small Western Slope growers, Plum Creek also farms more than 55 acres, planted in Colorado's high-altitude wine-growing regions centered in Palisade and Paonia. Plum Creek features a variety of wines sure to appeal to all tastes: Sauvignon Blanc, Cabernet Sauvignon, Chardonnay, Riesling, Merlot, and our premium Grand Mesa and dessert wines, Somerset and Late Harvest Sauvignon Blanc. Plum Creek is also famed for the Palisade series of wine: Festival, Palisade Rosé and Palisade Red.

We feature a knowledgeable staff in an inviting, spacious tasting room filled with fine art and antiques, along with outdoor sculpture, to enhance the wine-tasting experience.

TASTING ROOM INFORMATION: Daily, from 10 a.m. to 5 p.m.

DIRECTIONS: From the intersection of I-70 and Exit #42 in Palisade: Head south on Elberta Avenue (37 3/10 Road); turn right (west) onto G Road/Hwy 6. Look for the winery's "Chardonnay Chicken" sculpture at the entrance.

OTHER AMENITIES AT WINERY: Unique gifts, wine-related merchandise, locally-made artisanal items

WINE AVAILABLE FOR PURCHASE OUTSIDE OF WINERY: Yes

OTHER TASTING ROOM LOCATIONS: Tewksbury and Company (see Front Range Region)

NOTES: _____

_____

_____

_____

REEDER MESA VINEYARDS

7799 Reeder Mesa Road, Whitewater, CO 81527
970-242-7468
reedermesawines.com
info@reedermesawines.com

OWNER: Doug and Kris Vogel

YEAR BEGAN OPERATION: 2000

AVERAGE CASES PRODUCED ANNUALLY: 1,200

WINES PRODUCED:
White: Gewürztraminer, Riesling
Red: Cabernet Franc, Cabernet Sauvignon, Merlot, Petit Sirah,
Petit Verdot, Syrah
Other: Blends called Lands End Wild Rosé, CabSyrah, Lands End Red,
Red Rocker Red; Port wine called Purple Haze.

MESSAGE FROM OWNER: Reeder Mesa Vineyards is a family-owned and operated vineyard and winery, where we strive to make your visit special. Our goal is to take the snobbery out of wine, one bottle at a time! We like to drink this stuff, not hide it away!

Savor our estate grown and bottled Riesling, as well as White Merlot, Cabernet Sauvignon, Merlot and the very special Lands End Red. Reeder Mesa also now offers a great answer to Port, Purple Haze.

We have over 400 Wine Club members who enjoy our Quarterly Wine "Pick Up Party" featuring food, barrel tasting and local entertainment. The business is growing and the quality of our wines is improving with each vintage.

Come visit and taste our delicious, award-winning wines!

TASTING ROOM INFORMATION: Wednesday through Saturday from 10 a.m. to 6 p.m., Sunday from noon to 4 p.m. Also, by appointment.

DIRECTIONS: From the intersection of Hwy 50 and Hwy 141, south of Grand Junction: Head south on Hwy 50; turn left (east) onto Reeder Mesa Road, just past Whitewater. We are 8 miles down the road. Turn right (south) at the Winery sign and drive down the dirt road to our entry gate.

OTHER AMENITIES AT WINERY: Wine-related and other merchandise for sale.

WINE AVAILABLE FOR PURCHASE OUTSIDE OF WINERY: Yes

OTHER TASTING ROOM LOCATIONS: No

NOTES: _____

_____

_____

_____

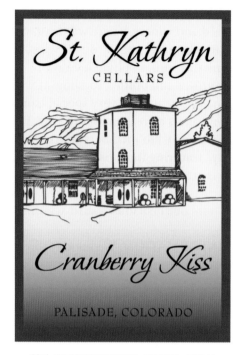

ST. KATHRYN CELLARS
785 Elberta Avenue, Palisade, CO 81526
970-464-9288
st-kathryn-cellars.com
Michael@talonwinebrands.com

OWNER: Glenn and Natalie Foster

YEAR BEGAN OPERATION: 1999

AVERAGE CASES PRODUCED ANNUALLY: 10,000 (for all 3 labels)

WINES PRODUCED:
White: Pinot Grigio, Riesling
Red: None
Other: Fruit wines–Apple Blossom, Golden Pear, Cherry, Peach
Passion, Concord Grape, Lavender, Strawberry Rhubarb, White Merlot,
Pomegranate, Cranberry Kiss, Blueberry Bliss, Elderberry, Sweet Scarlet,
and Merlot Port

MESSAGE FROM OWNER: St. Kathryn Cellars is owned and operated by Glenn and Natalie Foster, who purchased it in 2008. The Fosters have been in the wine industry since 1993, as Glenn's father founded and ran Ravenswood Winery in California for approximately 30 years.

St. Kathryn Cellars is famous for its fruit wines. Although there are a few grape wines, the most popular labels are Pomegranate, Strawberry Rhubarb, Cranberry Kiss, Blueberry Bliss, Peach Passion, and the new Lavender wine. While these wines are uncommon, they are also uncommonly delicious!

TASTING ROOM INFORMATION: Daily, from 10 a.m. to 5 p.m. During the summer, Friday and Saturday to 6 p.m.

DIRECTIONS: From I-70 at Exit #42: Head south on Elberta Avenue (37 3/10 Road). We are on the right.

OTHER AMENITIES AT WINERY: The Colorado Fudge Factory, where we offer hundreds of flavors and free tastes! A large gift shop stocked with wine paraphernalia.

WINE AVAILABLE FOR PURCHASE OUTSIDE OF WINERY: Yes

OTHER TASTING ROOM LOCATIONS: Talon Winery and Meadery of the Rockies (see Grand Valley Region); Honeyville Tasting Room (see Four Corners Region)

NOTES: _____

_____

_____

_____

TALON WINERY

785 Elberta Avenue, Palisade, CO 81526
970-464-9288
talonwineryco.com
Michael@talonwinebrands.com

OWNER: Glenn and Natalie Foster

YEAR BEGAN OPERATION: 2005

AVERAGE CASES PRODUCED ANNUALLY: 10,000 (for all 3 labels)

WINES PRODUCED:
White: Riesling
Red: Cabernet Sauvignon, Merlot
Other: Blends called Wingspan White, Rock Red, Wingspan Red, Rosato; Aquilla, a dessert wine

MESSAGE FROM OWNER: Talon Winery was founded by Glenn and Natalie Foster in 2005 when they opened a small, retail wine shop and produced a limited amount of wine in the back room. After three years, they needed to expand capacity, so they moved their operations to Palisade and acquired two other brands.

The Talon wines are devoted to locally-grown grape wines of the highest quality. We currently offer eight distinct varieties of wine: Wingspan White, Wingspan Red, Merlot, Cabernet Sauvignon, Rosato, Riesling and Aquila Dessert, a port-styled dessert wine, regularly winning numerous national and international awards.

TASTING ROOM INFORMATION: Daily, from 10 a.m. to 5 p.m. During the summer, Friday and Saturday to 6 p.m.

DIRECTIONS: From I-70 at Exit #42: Head south on Elberta Avenue (37 3/10 Road). We are on the right.

OTHER AMENITIES AT WINERY: The Colorado Fudge Factory, where we offer hundreds of flavors and free tastes! A large gift shop stocked with wine paraphernalia.

WINE AVAILABLE FOR PURCHASE OUTSIDE OF WINERY: Yes

OTHER TASTING ROOM LOCATIONS: St. Kathryn Cellars and Meadery of the Rockies (see Grand Valley Region); Honeyville Tasting Room (see Four Corners Region)

NOTES: _____

_____

_____

_____

TWO RIVERS WINERY

2087 Broadway Road, Grand Junction, CO 81507
970-255-1471 or 866-312-9463
tworiverswinery.com
info@tworiverswinery.com

OWNER: Robert "Bob" and Billie Witham

YEAR BEGAN OPERATION: 1999

AVERAGE CASES PRODUCED ANNUALLY: 14,000-16,000

WINES PRODUCED:
White: Chardonnay, Riesling
Red: Cabernet Sauvignon, Merlot, Syrah
Other: Vintner's Blend, Ruby Port

MESSAGE FROM OWNER: This family-operated boutique winery, offers wines from the noble varieties. Chateau deux Fleuves Vineyards (translated House on Two Rivers), encompasses 11 acres of estate-grown Chardonnay, Cabernet Sauvignon and Merlot grapes. In addition to estate-grown grapes, local grapes are purchased through contracts with other Colorado growers. The state-of-the-art winery is positioned in the center of the vineyard.

Great care and thought has been given to equip the crush area, fermentation room and cellar so that a high level of quality is maintained when taking the grapes from harvest, through fermentation, aging and bottling. While these meticulous practices have been implemented to enhance the complexity of the wine, there remains openness to innovation, which enables the winery to be responsive to its customers. This process is essential in achieving our three goals: Premium Wines, Consistency and Predictability and Customer Participation.

TASTING ROOM INFORMATION: Monday through Saturday from 10:30 a.m. to 6 p.m., Sunday from noon to 5 p.m.

DIRECTIONS: From the intersection of I-70 and Exit #28 (Redlands Parkway): Head south on Redlands Parkway; turn right (northwest) onto Broadway/Hwy 340. The winery is 2 miles up the road on left. (Note: GPS users should use Hwy 340 rather than Broadway.)

OTHER AMENITIES AT WINERY: Event Center, which can host a variety of functions and contains a fully-equipped catering kitchen. Available at our Wine Country Inn are ten upscale, guest rooms featuring unique, French-country décor and outstanding hospitality.

WINE AVAILABLE FOR PURCHASE OUTSIDE OF WINERY: Yes

OTHER TASTING ROOM LOCATIONS: No

NOTES: _____

_____

_____

_____

VARAISON VINEYARDS AND WINERY

405 W. 1st Street, Palisade, CO 81526
970-464-4928
varaisonvineyards.com
info@varaisonvineyards.com

OWNER: Ron and Kristin West

YEAR BEGAN OPERATION: 2001

AVERAGE CASES PRODUCED ANNUALLY: 12,000

WINES PRODUCED:
White: Creme Brûlée Chardonnay, Cuveé Blanc Chardonnay, Unoaked Chardonnay
Red: Bin 405 Merlot, Bin 3115 Merlot, Cuveé Noir
Other: Black Muscato Rosé, Black Muscato D'Asti Sparkling wine, Mimosa Orange Muscato Chardonnay - Methode Champenoise Sparkling wine

MESSAGE FROM OWNER: Varaison Vineyards and Winery is a family-owned boutique winery specializing in the production of premium quality estate wines. Located in Palisade, our state-of-the-art facility produces predominantly Old World style Burgundy, Bordeaux and Italian varietals as well as sparkling wines that are produced both method Charmat and Methode Champenoise. Varaison strives to allow the expression of the terroir unique to the Grand Valley AVA, by growing grapes that are herbicide- and pesticide-free, in support of sustainable agricultural practices.

Our company and staff are dedicated to enhancing the wine tasting experience by providing personalized education and knowledge to each valued guest. Varaison provides a distinctive venue, experience and opportunity to explore Colorado wines.

A 100-year-old Victorian tasting room and formal English rose garden offer a unique atmosphere for a relaxing and informative visit.

TASTING ROOM INFORMATION: Daily, from 10 a.m. to 5 p.m.

DIRECTIONS: From I-70 at Exit #42: Head south on Elberta Avenue (37 3/10 Road); turn left (east) onto 1st Avenue.

OTHER AMENITIES AT WINERY: The Palisade Pavilion accommodates up to 250 people for any event need and includes a catering kitchen. The Walking Gardens features over 1,500 David Austin Old English Roses.

WINE AVAILABLE FOR PURCHASE OUTSIDE OF WINERY: No

OTHER TASTING ROOM LOCATIONS: No

NOTES: _____

_____

_____

_____

WHITEWATER HILL VINEYARDS

220 32 Road, Grand Junction, CO 81503
Mailing address: 130 31 Road, Grand Junction, CO 81503
970-434-6868
whitewaterhill.com
info@whitewaterhill.com

OWNER: Nancy Janes and John Behrs

YEAR BEGAN OPERATION: 2004

AVERAGE CASES PRODUCED ANNUALLY: 2,000

WINES PRODUCED:
White: 'No Oak' Chardonnay, Gewürztraminer, Riesling, Viognier,
White Merlot
Red: Cabernet Franc, Cabernet Sauvignon, Merlot, Shiraz,
Other: Blends called Ethereal, Muscat Canelli, Sweetheart Red,
Crag Crest Ruby Classico; Ice wines

MESSAGE FROM OWNER: Whitewater Hill Vineyards is a family-owned and operated vineyard and winery, located in Grand Junction, Colorado. The husband and wife team of John Behrs and Nancy Janes left the high tech industry in Boulder in 1998 to grow grapes in the Grand Valley. John concentrates on the grape growing in the summer, and helps winemaker Nancy in the cellar during the winter.

They produce ten different wine grape varieties on 37 acres in the Grand Valley, growing both for other wineries and for their own small lot production. They also make 16 different award-winning wines with 100% Colorado grown grapes. Their wines range in style from full-bodied, dry wines, to elegant and fruity semi-sweet and dessert wines... "handgrown, handpicked, handcrafted."

TASTING ROOM INFORMATION: Summer, Monday through Friday from noon to 6 p.m., Saturday and Sunday from 10 a.m. to 6 p.m.; Winter, Friday through Sunday from noon to 6 p.m.

DIRECTIONS: From the intersection of I-70 and Exit #37 in Grand Junction: Head south on I-70 Business; turn left (south) onto 32 Road. The winery is 4 miles on 32 Road.

OTHER AMENITIES AT WINERY: Wine-related merchandise

WINE AVAILABLE FOR PURCHASE OUTSIDE OF WINERY: Yes

OTHER TASTING ROOM LOCATIONS: No

NOTES: _____

_____

_____

_____

GRAND VALLEY REGION

What Else To See & Do

Allen Unique Autos Showroom & Gallery   allenuniqueautos.com
"Beep, Beep"...take a look at this private automobile collection selected by Tammy Allen.

Bananas Fun Park   bananasfunpark.com
Let your kids (or your inner child) go wild and unwind through mini golf, bumper boats, an inflatable play land, batting cages, go karts and laser tag.

Colorado National Monument   nps.gov/colm
Can a rock really balance? View breathtaking scenery and captivating landscapes of towering cliffs, deep canyons, balancing rocks and giant monoliths on the 23-mile Rim Rock Drive. Find sightseeing, hiking, biking, and ranger-led programs at the Monument.

Farmers Market   townofpalisade.org & downtowngj.org
From mid-June through mid-September, these weekly events offer much more than just produce. Visit these websites for more information.

Grand Mesa   see the Internet for various websites
Ever been on the world's largest flat-top mountain? Grand Mesa offers a variety of outdoor activities ranging from sightseeing, hiking, biking and fishing during the summer and fall. In the winter, activities include crosscountry skiing, snowshoeing and snowmobiling. Powderhorn Mountain Resort offers downhill skiing and summer activities (www.powderhorn.com). A 63-mile drive takes you over the Mesa from the Grand Valley into Delta and Montrose Counties, with numerous scenic stops along the way.

Museum of Western Colorado   museumofwesternco.com
Become a paleontologist for the day at the Museum of Western Colorado and discover what this area was like years ago. There are three major museum facilities: Museum of the West, Dinosaur Journey Museum and Cross Orchards Historic Site.

- **Museum of the West** takes you back to western Colorado a thousand years ago, and includes Native American pottery, treasures from a Spanish merchant ship and a re-creation of a pioneer town.

- **Dinosaur Journey Museum** provides visitors the opportunity to examine dinosaur fossils, see a working paleontology lab and experience a simulated earthquake. Dinosaur Digs offers halfday to 5-day paleontology expeditions where you can explore for fossils at a dinosaur quarry.

- **Cross Orchards Historic Site** transports you to the early 1900s in the Grand Valley. Your experience will be enhanced by the costumed interpreters.

Outdoor Activities   trails.com or co.blm.gov/rectrails.htm

Hike to the top of the Book Cliff Mountain's highest peak, Mt. Garfield, and be rewarded with spectacular views. Like anywhere in Colorado, the Grand Valley region offers numerous hiking and biking trails, which are detailed at these two websites. And don't forget, you can always bike to the wineries! Grand Junction, Fruita and Palisade all offer city parks, swimming pools and skateparks, which can be found on each city's website.

SunCrest Orchard Alpacas   suncrestorchardalpacas.net

Need a sweater anyone? At this unique farm find out how alpaca fur is changed into fiber and manufactured into yarn.

Western Colorado Botanical Gardens   wcbotanic.org

Experience the beauty of nature at the Western Colorado Botanical Gardens and Butterfly House. The facility offers a butterfly exhibit and over 600 tropical plants from around the world. WCBG offers both indoor viewing and activities, as well as numerous outdoor gardens.

Western Colorado Center for the Arts   gjartcenter.org

Enjoy the arts? The Western Colorado Center for the Arts provides exhibits, displays and educational programs to promote the enjoyment and understanding of the arts.

For further information, please visit these websites:
visitgrandjunction.com   gjchamber.org
palisadecoc.com   fruitachamber.org

Delta & Montrose, West Elks Region

Wine Fact

In ancient Babylon, the bride's father would supply his son-in-law with all the mead (fermented honey beverage) he could drink for a month after the wedding. Because their calendar was lunar or moon-based, this period of free mead was called the "honey month;" what we now call the "honeymoon."

http://www.weddingnight.com/
advice/history-of-honeymoons.html

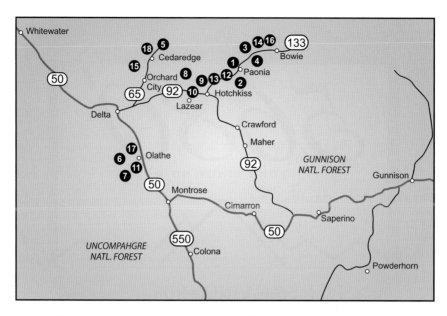

Delta & Montrose, West Elks Region Wineries

1. 5680' Vineyards
2. Alfred Eames Cellars
3. Azura Cellars and Gallery
4. Black Bridge Winery
5. Blossomwood Cidery
6. Cottonwood Cellars
7. Garrett Estate Vineyards
8. Jack Rabbit Hill
9. Leroux Creek Vineyards
10. Liliputian Winery
11. Mountain View Winery
12. North Fork Cellars
13. S. Rhodes Vineyard
14. Stone Cottage Cellars
15. Stoney Mesa Winery
16. Terror Creek Winery
17. The Olathe Winery
18. Woody Creek Cellars

5680' VINEYARDS
14652 Peony Lane, Paonia, CO 81428
970-527-6476
5680vineyards.com
robkimball7@hotmail.com

OWNER: Rob Kimball

YEAR BEGAN OPERATION: 2005

AVERAGE CASES PRODUCED ANNUALLY: 250-350

WINES PRODUCED:
White: Chardonnay
Red: Pinot Noir, Syrah
Other: Red blend; Dessert wine

MESSAGE FROM OWNER: Crisp mountain air, clear intense sunlight and pure water of the Colorado high country combine to provide our grapes with one of the most unique growing conditions in the world. Our vineyard sits at 5,680 feet, within the West Elks AVA, the highest recognized wine-growing elevation in the United States.

TASTING ROOM INFORMATION: By appointment only

DIRECTIONS: From the intersection of Hwy 133 and Hwy 187: Head south on Hwy 187 (Grand Avenue) through downtown Paonia; turn right (southwest) onto First Street (changes name to County Road J.75 Drive); turn right (northwest) onto Peony Lane.

OTHER AMENITIES AT WINERY: N/A

WINE AVAILABLE FOR PURCHASE OUTSIDE OF WINERY: Yes

OTHER TASTING ROOM LOCATIONS: Redstone Company Store (see Mountain Region)

NOTES: _____

_____

_____

_____

ALFRED EAMES CELLARS
11931 4050 Road, Paonia, CO 81428
970-527-3269
alfredeamescellars.com
info@alfredeamescellars.com

OWNER: Alfred Eames

YEAR BEGAN OPERATION: 1998

AVERAGE CASES PRODUCED ANNUALLY: 1,500

WINES PRODUCED:
White: None
Red: Pinot Noir, Syrah, Tempranillo
Other: Red blends called Collage and Sangre del Sol

MESSAGE FROM OWNER: My Estate bottled wine is Pinot Noir. My other wines are made from grapes grown on nearby Colorado vineyards, including the blends of Cabernet Franc, Cabernet Sauvignon, Carmine, Merlot, Syrah and Tempranillo.

TASTING ROOM INFORMATION: By appointment only

DIRECTIONS: From Hwy 133 near Paonia at the Stop and Save Gas Station on Hwy 133: Turn east onto Samuel Wade Road (changes to 3rd Street); turn right (south) onto Onarga Avenue (changes to Lamborn Mesa Road); keep straight onto 4100 Road; turn right (west) onto Stewart Mesa Road; keep straight onto 4050 Road. (map available on website)

OTHER AMENITIES AT WINERY: N/A

WINE AVAILABLE FOR PURCHASE OUTSIDE OF WINERY: Yes

OTHER TASTING ROOM LOCATIONS: Redstone Company Store (see Mountains Region)

NOTES: _____

_____

_____

_____

AZURA CELLARS AND GALLERY
16764 Farmers Mine Road, Paonia, CO 81428
970-390-4251
AzuraCellars.com
AzuraPaonia@aol.com

OWNER: Ty and Helen Gillespie

YEAR BEGAN OPERATION: 2007

AVERAGE CASES PRODUCED ANNUALLY: 175

WINES PRODUCED:
White: Pinot Gris, Riesling
Red: Merlot, Syrah
Other: None

MESSAGE FROM OWNER: Helen and Ty Gillespie are artists and sailors. Having completed an around-the-world cruise, they have settled down to produce world class art and boutique wines at the winery in Paonia. The stunning views and extraordinary architecture of the winery combine with boutique wines and exceptional art to make a visit to Azura Cellars an unforgettable experience!

TASTING ROOM INFORMATION: Memorial Day through the end of October, daily, from 11 a.m. to 6 p.m.

DIRECTIONS: From the intersection of Hwy 133 and Hwy 187 near Paonia: Head northeast on Hwy 133; turn left (north) onto Farmers Mine Road. The winery is about 1 mile from the Hwy 133 turnoff.

OTHER AMENITIES AT WINERY: Art Gallery and a wedding venue

WINE AVAILABLE FOR PURCHASE OUTSIDE OF WINERY: No

OTHER TASTING ROOM LOCATIONS: No

NOTES: _____

_____

_____

_____

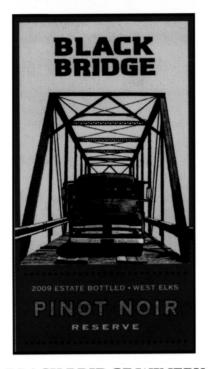

BLACK BRIDGE WINERY

15836 Black Bridge Road, Paonia, CO 81428
970-527-6838
blackbridgewinery.com
leeb@orchardvalleyfarms.com

OWNER: Lee and Kathy Bradley

YEAR BEGAN OPERATION: 2004

AVERAGE CASES PRODUCED ANNUALLY: 1,200

WINES PRODUCED:
White: Chardonnay, Riesling
Red: Merlot, Pinot Noir
Other: Blends called Breaker Row Red, Farmers Ditch Red

MESSAGE FROM OWNER: Western Colorado's terrain and weather have produced an ideal grape–growing region for more than a century. Nationally, Colorado is considered one of the finest emerging wine areas. Here in the West Elks, Orchard Valley Farms has been supplying some of Delta County's finest wineries with grapes since 1997.

In 2005 we introduced the premier vintage of our own wines. Named for the nearby historic bridge, Black Bridge Winery produces a limited number of wines each year. Our offerings include classic reds and red blends of Pinot Noir, Merlot, Syrah and Cabernet Sauvignon, and whites of Chardonnay and Riesling. Some are big, some are fruity, and all are delicious. Our Colorado wines are made in limited quantities, so stop by to sample and purchase in our tasting room, or shop year 'round online.

TASTING ROOM INFORMATION: Memorial Weekend through Halloween, daily from 10 a.m. to 6 p.m.

DIRECTIONS: From the intersection of Hwy 133 and Hwy 187 near Paonia: Head north on Hwy 133; turn right (east) onto Black Bridge Road, which is approximately 1 mile north of Paonia.

OTHER AMENITIES AT WINERY: An outside venue, which can accommodate up to 50 people

WINE AVAILABLE FOR PURCHASE OUTSIDE OF WINERY: Yes

OTHER TASTING ROOM LOCATIONS: Colorado Homestead Ranches (see Delta/Montrose and West Elks AVA Region) and Redstone Company Store (see Mountains Region)

NOTES: _____

_____

_____

_____

BLOSSOMWOOD CIDERY

794 NE Indian Camp Avenue, Cedaredge, CO 81413

970-856-3220

blossomwoodcidery.com

info@blossomwoodcidery.com

OWNER: Shawn and Janese Carney

YEAR BEGAN OPERATION: 2005

AVERAGE CASES PRODUCED ANNUALLY: 1,000

WINES PRODUCED:
White: None
Red: None
Other: Hard Ciders and Perry

MESSAGE FROM OWNER: Blossomwood Cidery is located on our farm in the Surface Creek Valley of Western Colorado, minutes from the Grand Mesa. We specialize in producing quality, artisan hard ciders and perry (fermented pear juice). We use strange and unusual cider varieties that have been all but forgotten in the United States, as well as European apple varieties that are bitter and high in tannin called "bittersweets." All fruit comes from our certified naturally-grown orchards.

TASTING ROOM INFORMATION: Friday through Sunday from 10 a.m. to 6 p.m.; Otherwise by appointment.

DIRECTIONS: From downtown Cedaredge: Head north on Hwy 65; turn right (east) onto NE Indian Camp Road.

OTHER AMENITIES AT WINERY: N/A

WINE AVAILABLE FOR PURCHASE OUTSIDE OF WINERY: Yes

OTHER TASTING ROOM LOCATIONS: Crested Butte, Aspen and Telluride Farmers Markets

NOTES: _____

_____

_____

_____

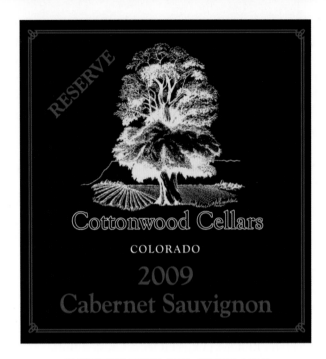

COTTONWOOD CELLARS

5482 Hwy 348, Olathe, CO 81425
Mailing address: PO Box 940, Olathe, CO 81425
970-323-6224
cottonwoodcellars.com
info@cottonwoodcellars.com
or cottonwoodwines@cs.com

OWNER: Keith and Diana Read

YEAR BEGAN OPERATION: 1994

AVERAGE CASES PRODUCED ANNUALLY: 3,500

WINES PRODUCED:
(Note: Not all wines are produced annually)
White: Chardonnay, White Pinot Noir
Red: Cabernet Franc, Cabernet Sauvignon, Reserve Cabernet
Sauvignon, Lemberger, Merlot, Reserve Merlot, Pinot Noir, Syrah
Other: Blend called Classic Blend

MESSAGE FROM OWNER: Owner's Keith and Diana Read retired from the Tech industry in California and started the Cottonwood Cellars winery in 1994. Keith apprenticed to a chemist in winemaking, as well as developing an extensive library on Enology and Viticulture. They planted 22.5 acres in seven varieties from 1995 to 2000 at 5,400' altitude, from which they produce approximately 3,500 cases per year. The red wines and Chardonnay (Sur Lees) are aged in a combination of new and neutral oak barrels from nine months to two years. The wines have superior quality, being well-balanced and varietal correct.

TASTING ROOM INFORMATION: Memorial Day weekend through October, Wednesday through Saturday from 11 a.m. to 5:30 p.m.; April through Memorial Day and November through December, Friday and Saturday from 11 a.m. to 5 p.m. Closed January through March, except by appointment only.

DIRECTIONS: From the intersection of Hwy 50 and Hwy 348 in Olathe: Head west on Hwy 348. Winery is 3.4 miles on the right side.

OTHER AMENITIES AT WINERY: Event facilities in tasting room and barrel room (75 people), front lawn (125 sit down) or 300 people for weddings, receptions, reunions. We also sell gift items.

WINE AVAILABLE FOR PURCHASE OUTSIDE OF WINERY: Yes

OTHER TASTING ROOM LOCATIONS: Colorado Winery Row and Coffee at the Point (see Front Range Region) and Cowbells and the Deersnake Gallery (see Pikes Peak Region)

NOTES: _____

_____

_____

_____

GARRETT ESTATE CELLARS

53582 Falcon Road, Olathe, CO 81425
Mailing address: 53716 Falcon Road, Olathe, CO 81425
970-901-5919
GarrettEstateCellars.com
Mitch@garrettestatecellars.com

OWNER: Dave and Pam Garrett

YEAR BEGAN OPERATION: 2006

AVERAGE CASES PRODUCED ANNUALLY: 4,200

WINES PRODUCED:
White: Chardonnay, Gewürztraminer, Pinot Gris, Riesling,
Sauvignon Blanc
Red: Cabernet Sauvignon, Merlot, Pinot Nior
Other: None

MESSAGE FROM OWNER: Our winery is a family-run operation, started by our parents in 2003, with our first vintage being introduced in 2008. We currently grow on 35 acres and are expanding to include an additional 20 acres. Our wines are traditional and of French styling. We are working to produce exceptional, inspiring, quality Colorado wines through excellence, integrity, simplicity and cooperation.

TASTING ROOM INFORMATION: Currently we do not have a tasting room; tours by appointment only.

DIRECTIONS: From the intersection of Hwy 50 and Hwy 348 in Olathe: Head west on Hwy 348; turn left (south) onto 5500 Road; turn right (west) onto Falcon Road; the road ends and our winery is on the left.

OTHER AMENITIES AT WINERY: N/A

WINE AVAILABLE FOR PURCHASE OUTSIDE OF WINERY: Yes

OTHER TASTING ROOM LOCATIONS: The Apple Shed Gallery and Delta Garden Center (see Delta/Montrose and West Elks AVA Region)

NOTES: _____

_____

_____

_____

JACK RABBIT HILL

26567 North Road, Hotchkiss, CO 81419
Mailing address: PO Box 2004, Hotchkiss, CO 81419
970-361-4249
jackrabbithill.com
lance@jackrabbithill.com

OWNER: Anna and Lance Hanson

YEAR BEGAN OPERATION: 2001

AVERAGE CASES PRODUCED ANNUALLY: 1,500

WINES PRODUCED:
White: Estate Chardonnay, Riesling
Red: Pinot Noir
Other: None

MESSAGE FROM OWNER: Jack Rabbit Hill is a diversified farm. This unique property includes 22 acres of vineyards, a 12-acre hopyard, an estate winery and the Peak Spirits distillery. The property is certified organic and biodynamic by Demeter.

TASTING ROOM INFORMATION: By appointment only

DIRECTIONS: From the intersection of Hwy 50 and Hwy 92 in Delta: Head east on Hwy 92 approximately 10 miles; turn left (north) onto Payne Siding Road (just past the town of Austin); turn right (east) onto North Road; turn left (north) to stay on North Road.

OTHER AMENITIES AT WINERY: N/A

WINE AVAILABLE FOR PURCHASE OUTSIDE OF WINERY: Yes

OTHER TASTING ROOM LOCATIONS: No

NOTES: _____

_____

_____

_____

LEROUX CREEK VINEYARDS

12388 3100 Road, Hotchkiss, CO 81419
970-872-4746
lerouxcreekinn.com
lerouxcreekinn@msn.com

OWNER: Yvon and Joanna

YEAR BEGAN OPERATION: 2005

AVERAGE CASES PRODUCED ANNUALLY: 600

WINES PRODUCED:
White: Cayuga White, Chambourcin
Red: Chambourcin, Merlot
Other: Rosé, Cherry wine and Port-style wine

MESSAGE FROM OWNER: Our vineyards cover four acres of our 54-acre farm. We grow two hybrid varieties—Chambourcin and Cayuga. All of our grapes are raised organically. The vineyard is in the West Elks AVA, and we share grapes, knowledge, experience and the occasional glass of wine with the other vintners in the area. We use local fruits when in season to make small quantities of delicious fruit wines.

Our grape harvest has become an annual event in our community, with folks from the surrounding area willing to help us when we pick our grapes. Everyone has a wonderful day with plenty of companionship, fresh air, fun, work, great food and a glass or two of current vintages. We certainly do appreciate their efforts that contribute so much to our harvest!

TASTING ROOM INFORMATION: Summer through fall, daily, from 11 a.m. to 5 p.m.

DIRECTIONS: From the intersection of Hwy 133 and Hwy 92 in Hotchkiss: Head west on Hwy 92; turn right (north) onto 3100 Road. The winery is approximately 2 miles down the road.

OTHER AMENITIES AT WINERY: Leroux Creek Inn & Vineyards Culinary Adventure stays; Wine experience featuring French-country gourmet lunch picnics and "Dining in the Vines" dinner series; Winery and vineyard tours, plus other fun activities; Leroux Creek Spa and products.

WINE AVAILABLE FOR PURCHASE OUTSIDE OF WINERY: Yes

OTHER TASTING ROOM LOCATIONS: No

NOTES: _____

_____

_____

_____

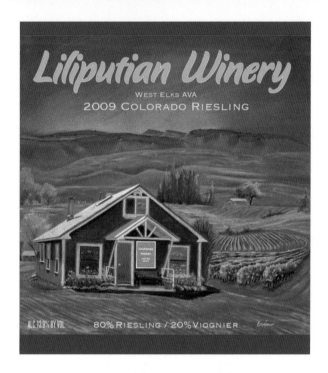

LILIPUTIAN WINERY

31428 Hwy 92, Hotchkiss, CO 81419
970-872-3019 or 800-665-1460
liliputianwinery.com
lisafairbank@gmail.com

OWNER: Lisa and Scott Fairbank

YEAR BEGAN OPERATION: 2008

AVERAGE CASES PRODUCED ANNUALLY: 500

WINES PRODUCED:
White: Riesling
Red: Cabernet Sauvignon
Other: ShangriLa (a ginger wine); Dessert wine, Apricot and
Cherry wines

MESSAGE FROM OWNER: Scott and Lisa Fairbank have been handcrafting fine wines in Hotchkiss for four years. Lisa enjoys creating unique wines from local grapes, fruits and herbs. Our specialty is Ginger Wine, known as ShangriLa. It is the only ginger wine being produced commercially in the United States and pairs beautifully with Sushi and other oriental foods.

TASTING ROOM INFORMATION: Monday through Saturday from 10 a.m. to 6 p.m., Sundays by appointment only.

DIRECTIONS: From the intersection of Hwy 133 and Hwy 92 in Hotchkiss: Head west on Hwy 92 approximately 3 miles. We are just past 3160 Road on Hwy 92.

OTHER AMENITIES AT WINERY: Box lunches and local food items for sale in our market, next to the winery.

WINE AVAILABLE FOR PURCHASE OUTSIDE OF WINERY: No

OTHER TASTING ROOM LOCATIONS: No

NOTES: _____

_____

_____

_____

MOUNTAIN VIEW WINERY

5859 58.25 Road, Olathe, CO 81425
970-323-6816
mountainviewwinery.com
mountainviewwinery@gmail.com

OWNER: Mike and Wendy Young

YEAR BEGAN OPERATION: 2000

AVERAGE CASES PRODUCED ANNUALLY: 1,000 - 3,000

WINES PRODUCED:
White: Chardonnay, Gewürztraminer, Pinot Grigio, Viognier
Red: Cabernet Sauvignon, Pinot Noir, Syrah
Other: Blends called Mountain Rosé, Ash Mesa, Chipeta White,
Uncompahgre, Dare Devil Red; Fruit and Dessert wines; Port wine

MESSAGE FROM OWNER: We are an orchard and a winery that have been in the family for over 50 years. Our goal is to take the hurry and hustle/bustle out of life for just a moment. We also sell "You-Pick" asparagus, apples, peaches, pears, plums and cherries in season. Come ready to sit and visit and enjoy!

TASTING ROOM INFORMATION: Monday through Saturday from 10 a.m. to 6 p.m. Our tasting room is open air, so come prepared in the winter months.

DIRECTIONS: From the intersection of Hwy 50 and Hwy 348 in Olathe: Head west on Hwy 348; turn right (north) onto 58.25 Road; the winery is at the first driveway on the left.

OTHER AMENITIES AT WINERY: We have outdoor options for hosting parties.

WINE AVAILABLE FOR PURCHASE OUTSIDE OF WINERY: Yes

OTHER TASTING ROOM LOCATIONS: Red Mountain Ranch (see Delta/Montrose and West Elks AVA Region)

NOTES: _____

_____

_____

_____

NORTH FORK CELLARS

39126 Hwy 133, Hotchkiss, CO 81419
Mailing address: PO Box 2012, Hotchkiss, CO 81419
970-527-1110
northforkcider.com
info@northforkcider.com

OWNER: Jeff Schwartz and Seth Schwartz

YEAR BEGAN OPERATION: 2009

AVERAGE CASES PRODUCED ANNUALLY: Information not Available

WINES PRODUCED:
White: None
Red: None
Other: Traditional Hard Cider, Spiced Hard Cider, Cherry Hard Cider

MESSAGE FROM OWNER: We produce a traditional, still farmhouse-style Dry Cider, made with 100% organic cider apples. It is handcrafted and all naturally fermented in small batches. A bouquet of apple blossom mingles with the subtle sweetness of apple and floral flavors. Our Hard Apple Cider is an excellent match for a hot summer night… Ah, who are we kidding? It tastes great and we drink it all the time!

Delicious Orchards, the home of North Fork Cellars, has a beautiful farm store with great local organic products, a café serving delicious food made from local ingredients and a campground nestled in the orchard. Additionally, guests can come by and hand pick organic cherries, pears, peaches and apples. Delicious Orchards and North Fork Cellars are proud to support local, sustainable agricultural and land stewardship.

TASTING ROOM INFORMATION: April to December, daily, from 9 a.m. to 5 p.m.

DIRECTIONS: Located on Hwy 133 one mile west of Paonia

OTHER AMENITIES AT WINERY: A café featuring local ingredients, an organic farm stand, camping, special events and U-Pick.

WINE AVAILABLE FOR PURCHASE OUTSIDE OF WINERY: Yes

OTHER TASTING ROOM LOCATIONS: No

NOTES: _____

_____

_____

_____

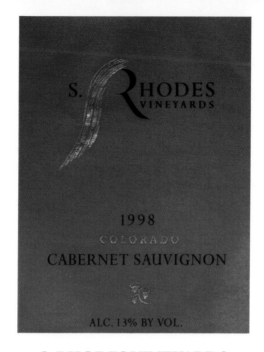

S. RHODES VINEYARDS

35837 Hanson Mesa Road, Hotchkiss, CO 81419
970-275-5969
Website: N/A
Email: N/A

OWNER: Steve Rhodes

YEAR BEGAN OPERATION: 1996

AVERAGE CASES PRODUCED ANNUALLY: Information not Available

WINES PRODUCED:
White: None
Red: Barbera, Claret, Merlot, Pinot Noir
Other: Gewürztraminer Ice wine

MESSAGE FROM OWNER: N/A

TASTING ROOM INFORMATION: Memorial Day through Labor Day, Wednesday through Sunday from noon to 6 p.m.

DIRECTIONS: From the intersection of Hwy 133 and Hwy 92 in Hotchkiss: Head north on Hwy 133 approximately 2 miles; turn left (northwest) onto Hanson Mesa Road. The winery is just down the road.

OTHER AMENITIES AT WINERY: N/A

WINE AVAILABLE FOR PURCHASE OUTSIDE OF WINERY: Yes

OTHER TASTING ROOM LOCATIONS: No

NOTES: _____

_____

_____

_____

STONE COTTAGE CELLARS

41716 Reds Road, Paonia, CO 81428
970-527-3444
stonecottagecellars.com
info@stonecottagecellars.com

OWNER: Karen and Brent Helleckson

YEAR BEGAN OPERATION: 2003

AVERAGE CASES PRODUCED ANNUALLY: 650-800

WINES PRODUCED:
White: Chardonnay, Gewürztraminer
Red: Merlot, Pinot Noir, Syrah
Other: Alpine Dessert wine

MESSAGE FROM OWNER: We are a small, intimate estate winery reminiscent of Old Europe. The winery and outbuildings are constructed of local fieldstone, and the wines are crafted with similar attention to traditional quality.

TASTING ROOM INFORMATION: Memorial Day through October, daily, from 11 a.m. to 6 p.m.

DIRECTIONS: From the intersection of Hwy 187 and Hwy 133 near Paonia: Head north on Hwy 133; turn left (north) at the second left, which is Garvin Mesa Road; turn left (west) onto Reds Road.

OTHER AMENITIES AT WINERY: Vineyard tours, Cellar tours, vacation rental property on site - "The Stone Cottage" (sleeps 4).

WINE AVAILABLE FOR PURCHASE OUTSIDE OF WINERY: Yes

OTHER TASTING ROOM LOCATIONS: No

NOTES: _____

_____

_____

_____

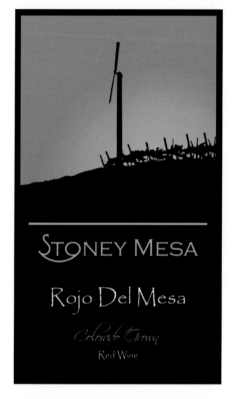

STONEY MESA WINERY
16199 Happy Hollow Road, Cedaredge, CO 81413
970-856-9463
stoneymesa.com
wine@stoneymesa.com

OWNER: Bret Neal

YEAR BEGAN OPERATION: 1990

AVERAGE CASES PRODUCED ANNUALLY: Information not Available

WINES PRODUCED:
White: Gewürztraminer, Pinot Gris, Riesling
Red: Cabernet Sauvignon, Merlot,
Other: Blend called Rojo del Mesa, Blush wine

MESSAGE FROM OWNER: Riesling is King at our modern facility, which utilizes proven Old World technology with modern equipment. We incorporate gentle fruit handling, temperature-controlled fermentation and small lot production into our wines.

Since starting in 1990, Stoney Mesa Winery has become a pioneer in the production of wine grapes and winemaking in Colorado. Our first vintage was released to the public in 1993 and, since then, we are highly regarded as one of the top white wine producers in the state.

Over the past 20 years, we have grown and expanded our facilities, production and vineyards but still focus on high quality wines at a great price. Stop by our winery or vineyard for tastings and tours.

TASTING ROOM INFORMATION: May through October, daily, from 11 a.m. to 5 p.m.; November through April, Monday through Saturday from 11 a.m. to 5 p.m., Sunday from noon to 3:30 p.m.

DIRECTIONS: From downtown Cedaredge on Hwy 65: Head south; turn right (west) onto SW 11th Avenue; turn left (south) onto Happy Hollow Road.

OTHER AMENITIES AT WINERY: Gift shop; available for event rental.

WINE AVAILABLE FOR PURCHASE OUTSIDE OF WINERY: Yes

OTHER TASTING ROOM LOCATIONS: No

NOTES: _____

_____

_____

_____

Terror Creek

2003

COLORADO

Riesling
·DRY·

PRODUCED AND BOTTLED BY TERROR CREEK WINERY
PAONIA, CO 81428   ALCOHOL 13.5% BY VOLUME   CONTAINS SULFITES

TERROR CREEK WINERY

17445 Garvin Mesa Road, Paonia, CO 81428
970-527-3484
terrorcreekwinery.com
jmath@paonia.com

OWNER: John and Joan Mathewson

YEAR BEGAN OPERATION: 1992

AVERAGE CASES PRODUCED ANNUALLY: 500 - 800

WINES PRODUCED:
White: Unoaked Chardonnay, Gewürztraminer, Riesling
Red: Pinot Noir
Other: Blend called Chalet

MESSAGE FROM OWNER: John Mathewson, a Colorado School of Mines graduate, and his wife Joan, a Colorado Woman's College graduate, found this wonderful piece of land in the 1980s. They started planting vines next to a small plot of Gewürztraminer, which had been planted in 1972 as a part of Colorado State University's "Four Corners Project."

Today, the grapes are handpicked and crafted into wine by enologist, Joan, whose diploma was earned at "L'Ecole Changins" in Nyon, Switzerland. The wines are European in style - clean, fruity and true to the grape varietal...Delicious!

TASTING ROOM INFORMATION: Memorial Day weekend through September, daily, 11 a.m. to 5 p.m.; October, Saturday and Sunday from 11 a.m. to 5 p.m.

DIRECTIONS: From the intersection of Hwy 133 and Hwy 187 in Paonia: Head north on Hwy 133; turn left (north) onto Garvin Mesa Road. Winery is at the end of the road.

OTHER AMENITIES AT WINERY: Lovely gardens with magnificent views of the valley and West Elk Mountains.

WINE AVAILABLE FOR PURCHASE OUTSIDE OF WINERY: Yes

OTHER TASTING ROOM LOCATIONS: No

NOTES: _____

_____

_____

_____

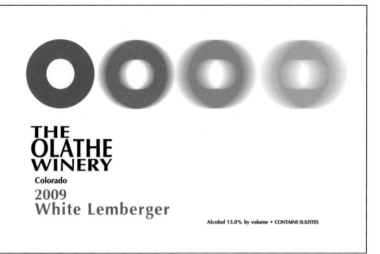

THE
OLATHE
WINERY
Colorado
2009
White Lemberger

Alcohol 13.0% by volume • CONTAINS SULFITES

THE OLATHE WINERY

5482 Hwy 348, Olathe, CO 81425
Mailing address: PO Box 940, Olathe, CO 81425
970-323-6224
cottonwoodcellars.com
info@cottonwoodcellars.com
or cottonwoodwines@cs.com

OWNER: Keith and Diana Read

YEAR BEGAN OPERATION: 1994

AVERAGE CASES PRODUCED ANNUALLY: 3,500

WINES PRODUCED:
(Note: Some wines are not produced annually)
White: Chardonnay, White Lemberger
Red: Cabernet Sauvignon, Lemberger, Merlot, Pinot Noir
Other: Blends called Claret, Pinolem

MESSAGE FROM OWNER: Owner's Keith and Diana Read retired from the Tech industry in California and started Cottonwood Cellars Winery in 1994. Keith apprenticed to a chemist in winemaking as well as developing an extensive library on Enology and Viticulture. They planted 22.5 acres in seven varieties from 1995 to 2000 at 5,400' altitude.

The red wines and Chardonnay (Sur Lees) are fermented slowly, under cool temperatures, and aged in a combination of new and neutral oak barrels from nine months to two years. White, off-dry wines are produced under strict temperature control producing very fruity wines at low residual sugar levels. The wines have superior quality being well-balanced and varietal correct.

TASTING ROOM INFORMATION: Memorial Day weekend through October, Wednesday through Saturday from 11 a.m. to 5:30 p.m.; April through Memorial Day and November through December, Friday and Saturday from 11 a.m. to 5 p.m. Closed January through March, except by appointment only.

DIRECTIONS: From the intersection of Hwy 50 and Hwy 348 in Olathe: Head west on Hwy 348. Winery is 3.4 miles on the right side.

OTHER AMENITIES AT WINERY: Event facilities in tasting room and barrel room (75 people), front lawn (125 sit down) or 300 people for weddings, receptions, reunions. We also sell gift items.

WINE AVAILABLE FOR PURCHASE OUTSIDE OF WINERY: Yes

OTHER TASTING ROOM LOCATIONS: Colorado Winery Row and Coffee at the Point (see Front Range Region) and Cowbells and the Deersnake Gallery (see Pikes Peak Region)

NOTES: _____

_____

_____

_____

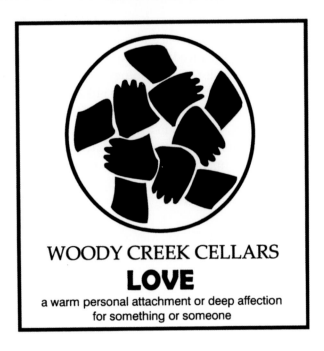

WOODY CREEK CELLARS
LOVE
a warm personal attachment or deep affection
for something or someone

WOODY CREEK CELLARS

Mailing address: PO Box 69, Austin, CO 81410
970-901-7575
woodycreekcellars.com
Email: N/A

OWNER: Kevin Doyle

YEAR BEGAN OPERATION: 2000

AVERAGE CASES PRODUCED ANNUALLY: 2,000

WINES PRODUCED:
White: None
Red: Cabernet Franc, Cabernet Sauvignon, Grenache, Merlot,
Pinot Noir, Sangiovese, Syrah, Tempranillo
Other: None

MESSAGE FROM OWNER: Woody Creek Cellars is dedicated to making fine natural wines with Old-World methods, using only Colorado's finest natural ingredients. We focus on small lot production and high quality. Guided by an ethos of simplicity, Woody Creek Cellars' handmade wines are made with primitive equipment.

Our wines are chemical-free, gravity flown, unfiltered and aged in French oak barrels. Woody Creek Cellars' wines are a benchmark for Colorado wines focusing on good quality at a great price. Our label features five interlocking hands, a symbol and reflection of owner/winemaker, Kevin Doyle's belief in a sense of community and strength through unity. When you stop by for a tasting, ask about our custom labeling on all of our wines!

TASTING ROOM INFORMATION: By appointment only

DIRECTIONS: Given at time of appointment reservation.

OTHER AMENITIES AT WINERY: N/A

WINE AVAILABLE FOR PURCHASE OUTSIDE OF WINERY: Yes

OTHER TASTING ROOM LOCATIONS: Palma Cigar (see Front Range Region)

NOTES: _____

_____

_____

_____

DELTA & MONTROSE, WEST ELKS REGION
What Else To See & Do

Black Canyon of the Gunnison National National Park   nps.gov/blca/index.htm

You take the South Rim and I'll take the North Rim, and both of us will see incredible sights! The park's many overlooks provide spectacular views of sheer, narrow canyon walls, which plummet to the Gunnison River. The roads can take you to several other recreation areas that border the park, and to the bottom of the canyon.

Curecanti National Recreation Area   nps.gov/cure/index.htm

Fishing, boating, hiking, scenic drives…Curecanti Recreation Area has it all! Experience the panoramic mesas, fjord-like reservoirs and steep, narrow canyons. Three reservoirs make up this area: Crystal, Morrow Point and Blue Mesa. And, in case you need a little help catching a fish, Federal and State fish hatcheries stock them with over three million fish each year! The Elk Creek Visitor Center provides valuable information.

Delta - City of Murals   deltacolorado.org/visitor.htm

Pick up a brochure at the Delta Visitor Center, which will guide you to several buildings that depict local scenes painted by area artists.

Delta County Historical Museum   deltacolorado.org/visitor.htm

Can you combine history and science in one place? You can at this museum, which features cultural and natural history of the area, as well as fossil, dinosaur and butterfly specimens.

Fort Uncompahgre   forttours.com

Take a step back in time to the 1800s when this living history museum was built. The Fort was originally used as a fur trapping and trading post. Today, guides dressed in period costumes provide a hands-on tour.

Grand Mesa   grandmesabyway.org / see the internet for websites

Ever been on the world's largest flat-top mountain? Grand Mesa offers a variety of outdoor activities ranging from sightseeing, hiking, biking and fishing during the summer and fall. In the winter, the activities include cross-country skiing, snowshoeing and snowmobiling. **Powderhorn Mountain Resort** offers downhill skiing and summer activities (**www.powderhorn.com**). A 63-mile drive takes you over the Mesa from Delta and Montrose Counties into the Grand Valley, offering numerous scenic stops along the way.

Morrow Point Boat Tours   nps.gov/cure/planyourvisit/boattour.htm
Travel into the Black Canyon of the Gunnison via a boat tour led by a park ranger. Learn about the geology, the dams and reservoirs and the wildlife.

Outdoor Activities
Outdoor activities abound throughout this area every season of the year.

- **Fishing**   nps.gov/cure/index.htm & visitmontrose.com
- **Hiking, Biking**   trails.com & numerous websites
- **Rafting**   visitmontrose.com
- **Winter Activities**   visitmontrose.com

Pioneer Town   pioneertown.org
What was life like in the late 1800s in Cedaredge, Colorado? Experience a bygone era at this reconstructed town where all the structures are either original restorations or authentic replicas. Over 20 buildings line the boardwalk and are packed with history.

The Creamery Arts Center   creameryartscenter.org
What does cream have to do with art? The 1930's Creamery Building has been renovated, and is now a cooperative featuring 100 area artists. Their work is displayed in a dramatic two-story gallery. They host a monthly Artist Reception with art, food, wine and beer. During the summer months visit their Farmers Market for local produce.

West Elk Scenic By-Way   gunnisoncrestedbutte.com/
                                 area-tour/west-elk-scenic-and-historic-byway
The By-Way provides 204-miles of incredible scenery, history of Western Colorado and a winery or two along the way! This roadway passes through rural, designated Wilderness and National Forest areas, providing you with potential glimpses of animals and wildflowers along the way.

For further information, please visit these websites:

deltacolorado.org/visitor.htm   visitmontrose.com
co.montrose.co.us   deltacountycolorado.com
cedaredgecolorado.com   hotchkisschamber.com
paoniachamber.com

Additional Tasting Locations

Colorado Homestead Ranches (Black Bridge Winery)
101 Grand Avenue, Paonia, CO 81428
970-527-7455
homesteadbeef.com
Owner: Co-op of six family ranches
Hours: Monday through Saturday from 9 a.m. to 5:30 p.m.

Delicious Orchards (North Fork Cellars, various other wineries)
39126 Hwy 133, Hotchkiss, CO 81419
970-527-1110
deliciousorchardstore.com
Owner: Jeff Schwartz
Hours: April through December, daily from 9 a.m. to 5 p.m.

Red Mountain Ranches (Mountain View Winery)
19458 Hwy 65, Cedaredge, CO 81413
970-856-3803
redmountainranches.com
Owner: Bob and Roxie Morris, Manuel and Loree Gutierrez
Hours: Mid-June through October, daily from 10 a.m. to 6 p.m.;
October through December, Monday through Saturday from 10 a.m.
to 5 p.m., Sunday from 11 a.m. to 4 p.m.; January through mid-June,
call ahead for hours.

The AppleShed Gallery(Garrett Estate Vineyards)
250 S. Grand Mesa Drive, Cedaredge, CO 81413
970-856-7007
theappleshed.net
Owner: Connie Williams
Hours: Monday through Friday from 9 a.m. to 5:30 p.m.,
Saturday and Sunday from 9 a.m. to 4 p.m.

The Delta Garden Center (Garrett Estate Vineyards)
1970 S. Main Street, Delta, CO 81416
970-874-9009
deltagardencenter.com
Owner: Dan and Connie Williams
Hours: Monday through Saturday from 9 a.m. to 5 p.m.,
Sunday from 9 a.m. to 4 p.m.

Four Corners Region

Wine Fact

In ancient Greece, a dinner host would take the first sip of wine to assure guests the wine was not poisoned, hence the phrase "drinking to one's health." "Toasting" started in ancient Rome when the Romans continued the Greek tradition but started dropping a piece of toasted bread into each wine glass to temper undesirable tastes or excessive acidity.

http://facts.randomhistory.com/ 2009/08/21_wine.html

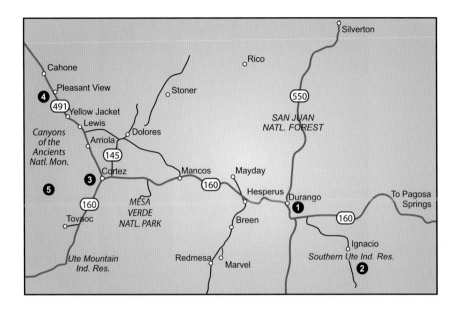

Four Corners Region Wineries

1. Four Leaves Winery
2. Fox Fire Farms
3. Guy Drew Vineyards
4. Pleasant View Winery
5. Sutcliffe Vineyards

FOUR LEAVES WINERY
528 Main Avenue, Durango, CO 81301
970-403-8182
fourleaveswinery.com
winery@winerymsprings.com

OWNER: Tracy and Dean Fagner

YEAR BEGAN OPERATION: 2011

AVERAGE CASES PRODUCED ANNUALLY: Information not Available

WINES PRODUCED:
White: Chardonnay, Pinot Grigio, Sauvignon Blanc
Red: Pinot Noir, Merlot, Sangiovese, Syrah
Other: Numerous red blends, Fruit wines, Port wines, Ice wine

MESSAGE FROM OWNER: Four Leaves Winery is a boutique winery located in downtown Durango. We import the highest quality grapes and then handcraft, blend and ferment all of our wines right in front of you! Want to create a custom blend that is all your own? Our staff can guide you through making your very own wine! In addition to having a custom blend, you can enjoy a bottling party with friends, and each bottle will have your own personalized label.

We are located right across the street from the Durango & Silverton Railroad Depot in downtown Durango. Drop in and enjoy a wine tasting, a glass of wine, or pick up a bottle before or after your train ride!

TASTING ROOM INFORMATION: Monday through Saturday from noon to 8 p.m., Sunday from noon to 7 p.m.

DIRECTIONS: Located in downtown Durango, across the street from the Durango & Silverton Narrow Gauge Railroad Depot.

OTHER AMENITIES AT WINERY: Wine-related merchandise and light appetizers. We are available for private parties, events and weddings. Art work is available for purchase. We allow our customers to make their own wine and bottle it when it is ready.

WINE AVAILABLE FOR PURCHASE OUTSIDE OF WINERY: Yes

OTHER TASTING ROOM LOCATIONS: D'Vine Wine - Manitou Springs (see Pikes Peak Region)

NOTES: _____

_____

_____

_____

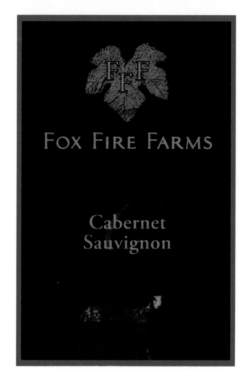

FOX FIRE FARMS

5513 County Road 321, Ignacio, CO 81137
970-563-4675
foxfirefarms.com
info@foxfirefarms.com

OWNER: Richard and Linda Parry

YEAR BEGAN OPERATION: 2009

AVERAGE CASES PRODUCED ANNUALLY: 500

WINES PRODUCED:
White: Chardonnay, Riesling
Red: Cabernet Sauvignon, Pinot Noir
Other: Blend called Fox Fire Red

MESSAGE FROM OWNER: Richard and Linda Parry are the owners and operators of Fox Fire Farms. The Parry family has been ranching and farming in Southwest Colorado since 1913. Despite the rapid commercial and residential development of Southwest Colorado, our farms are a true haven to the people who live and work here, our livestock and the abundant wildlife. We have developed a local and national reputation as practitioners of sustainable agriculture, and our livestock is certified organic.

A few years ago, we branched out into viticulture and have begun producing delicious wines. Please stop by for a taste!

TASTING ROOM INFORMATION: May through October, daily from 1 to 6 p.m. Off-season by appointment only.

DIRECTIONS: From downtown Ignacio: Head east on Hwy 151; turn right (south) onto Hwy 321. We are 4 miles from the intersection of Hwy 151 and Hwy 321.

OTHER AMENITIES AT WINERY: Wine-related merchandise and other Colorado wines available for tasting. We are available for private parties, events, meetings and weddings, which can be catered.

WINE AVAILABLE FOR PURCHASE OUTSIDE OF WINERY: Yes

OTHER TASTING ROOM LOCATIONS: Durango Coffee Company (see Four Corners Region)

NOTES: _____

_____

_____

_____

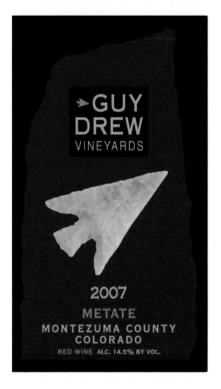

GUY DREW VINEYARDS

19891 Road G, Cortez, CO 81321
Mailing address: PO Box 1750, Cortez, CO 81321
970-565-9211
guydrewvineyards.com
guydrew@q.com

OWNER: Guy and Ruth Drew

YEAR BEGAN OPERATION: 2000

AVERAGE CASES PRODUCED ANNUALLY: 3,500

WINES PRODUCED:
White: Unoaked Chardonnay, Gewürztraminer, Riesling, Viognier
Red: Baco Noir, Cabernet Sauvignon, Merlot, Syrah
Other: Meritage, Port wine

MESSAGE FROM OWNER: We focus on fruit grown in Colorado. We have Estate vineyards and purchase from six growers in the Four Corners area that grow for us. We also source fruit from Palisade, primarily from Talbott Farms. Our state-of-the-art winemaking facility allows us to make premium Colorado wines at reasonable prices. We have won many awards from international wine competitions and have had accolades from national media.

The Four Corners region and Montezuma County have incredible potential for growing premium wine grapes. There are vineyards from just over 5,000' up to 7,000' in elevation that give us diverse growing micro-climates, and creates the opportunity to grow many different varieties.

TASTING ROOM INFORMATION: Daily, from noon to 5 p.m.

DIRECTIONS: From downtown Cortez: Head south on Hwy 160/491; turn right (west) onto Road G; the winery is 4 miles down the road.

OTHER AMENITIES AT WINERY: Bistro tables in our courtyard (bring your own food)

WINE AVAILABLE FOR PURCHASE OUTSIDE OF WINERY: Yes

OTHER TASTING ROOM LOCATIONS: No

NOTES: _____

_____

_____

_____

PLEASANT VIEW VINEYARDS

22970 County Road 10, Pleasant View, CO 81331
Mailing address: PO Box 249, Pleasant View, CO 81331
970-562-4553
pleasantviewvineyards.info
pvvineyards@fone.net

OWNER: Elizabeth and Allan Bleak

YEAR BEGAN OPERATION: 2011

AVERAGE CASES PRODUCED ANNUALLY: 100

WINES PRODUCED:
White: Chardonnay
Red: Pinot Noir
Other: None

MESSAGE FROM OWNER: Elizabeth and Allan Bleak started building their home in Pleasant View, Colorado in 1997 and became residents in 2000. The vineyard and orchard were established in 2001, with the help of their family and friends. Many years of thoughtful trial and error and perseverance have culminated into a love of viticulture, and naturally the end product, wine. We hope you enjoy our wines as much as we have enjoyed and loved our journey to bring them to you!

Pleasant View Vineyards, is nestled among old-growth juniper and pinion forests adjacent to the Canyons of the Ancients. This Single Vineyard Canyon Country wine truly has captured the same delicate, yet very robust, essence that is experienced when visiting the surrounding Canyons and National Monuments. Our organic growing practices have been maintained since the initial planting in 2001, and we do not use any chemicals. We conserve water, utilizing a drip irrigation system, and in keeping with sustainability and ecological considerations, all water and pressed grape skins are worked back into the soil from which they came.

TASTING ROOM INFORMATION: By appointment only

DIRECTIONS: From the intersection of Hwy 184 and Hwy 491 north of Cortez: Head north on Hwy 491; turn left (west) at MM45 onto BB Road; turn left (south) onto County Road 10 (approximately 5 miles). The winery is 3 miles down the road on left (white gates, red flowers on gates).

OTHER AMENITIES AT WINERY: N/A

WINE AVAILABLE FOR PURCHASE OUTSIDE OF WINERY: Yes

OTHER TASTING ROOM LOCATIONS: No

NOTES: _____

_____

_____

_____

SUTCLIFFE VINEYARDS
12174 Road G, Cortez, CO 81321
970-565-0825
sutcliffewines.com
info@sutcliffewines.com

OWNER: John Sutcliffe

YEAR BEGAN OPERATION: 1999

AVERAGE CASES PRODUCED ANNUALLY: 3,000

WINES PRODUCED:
White: Chardonnay, Gewürztraminer, Pinot Gris, Riesling,
Sauvignon Blanc, Viognier
Red: Cabernet Franc, Cabernet Sauvignon, Cinsaut, Grenache,
Merlot, Pinot Noir, Petit Verdot, Syrah, Zinfandel
Other: Blends called Bodysgallen, Down Canyon, Field Blend,
Hafoty Fawr and Trawsfynydd and Ael y Bryn Rosé

MESSAGE FROM OWNER: The first vines were planted in 1995 on the architect's aesthetic whim, with no lofty dream of having a vineyard. The first harvest was in 1999, and the wines produced were marketed in 2001. They were small bottlings of Merlot, Cabernet Franc and Syrah.

Our current winemaker, Joe Buckel, joined us from the Sonoma Valley after a career with BR Cohn, Flowers and Rutz. He loves the wines of Burgundy and the Rhone, and he exercises both restraint and patience in making his elegant wines. We are invariably told that our wines have an Old World style.

As an ex-restaurateur, John Sutcliffe from the very start was most comfortable selling to restaurants, and our penetration of that market in Aspen, Telluride, Vail, New York and restaurants on the West Coast was new for Colorado wines. We also raise livestock, cut hay and grow orchard fruit as well as grapes.

TASTING ROOM INFORMATION: Daily, from noon to 5 p.m.

DIRECTIONS: From the intersection of Hwy 491 and Hwy 160 in Cortez: Head south on Hwy 419/160; turn right (west) onto Road G/County Road G at the Cortez Municipal Airport; the winery is approximately 10 miles down the road.

OTHER AMENITIES AT WINERY: Annual harvest dinner at our farm at Dunton Hot Springs in Dolores.

WINE AVAILABLE FOR PURCHASE OUTSIDE OF WINERY: Yes

OTHER TASTING ROOM LOCATIONS: Sutcliffe Vineyards Tasting Room and West Fork Gallery (see Four Corners Region) and Shangri-La (see Front Range Region)

NOTES: _____

_____

_____

_____

FOUR CORNERS REGION
What Else To See & Do

Archeological Sites — see Tourism & Chamber of Commerce websites below

Want to know what the Ancestral Pueblo people used a kiva for? The Four Corners region of southwest Colorado is an archaeological Mecca! Here you can visit numerous ruins, with major sites located at Mesa Verde, Hovenweep and Ute Mountain Tribal Park.

- **Mesa Verde National Park** — nps.gov/meve/index.htm
  Visit some of the most well-preserved archeological sites in the United States and learn about the people who lived there for over 700 years. Experience breathtaking vistas on your scenic drive or partake in self-guided and ranger-led tours through many of the cliff dwellings.

- **Hovenweep** — nps.gov/hove
  Walk among multi-storied towers at this Monument that protects six prehistoric, Puebloan-era villages that were occupied from approximately 500 to 1300 AD. Square Tower offers a Visitor Center and interpretive trail.

- **Ute Mountain Tribal Park** — utemountainute.com/tribalpark
  Take a guided tour with a Ute tribal member, visit an ancestral pueblo and see petroglyphs and artifacts at this fascinating site.

Durango & Silverton Narrow Gauge Railroad — durangotrain.com

Take a ride on this historic train through spectacular scenery, traveling round-trip from Durango to Silverton. The vintage, steam locomotive train operates year-round. Advance reservations are <u>highly</u> recommended.

Durango Mountain Resort — durangomountainresort.com

Take in the magnificent views of the San Juan Mountains while enjoying winter or summer activities at Purgatory at Durango Mountain Resort. During the winter months, ski on some of the 85 downhill trails or enjoy snowcat trips, snowmobiling, cross-country skiing and sleigh rides. During the summer, take a scenic chairlift ride, go horseback riding, hiking or mountain biking, or experience the thrill of a zipline.

Four Corners   explorefourcorners.com

Here is your chance to stand in four states at the same time: Colorado, New Mexico, Arizona and Utah! Nowhere else in the United States can you experience this.

Gambling   skyutecasino.com

Try your luck at the Sky Ute Casino located on the Southern Ute Indian Reservation near Ignacio.

Highway 550 - San Juan Skyway & Million Dollar Highway

Fasten your seat belts and get your camera ready, as this spectacular drive with its breathtaking views takes you from the Four Corners area into other southwest Colorado towns such as Silverton, Ouray, Ridgeway and Telluride.

Hot Springs   see information in **Mountain Region** section

Outdoor Activities - An adventure awaits you!

- **Hiking and Biking**   trails.com or co.blm.gov/rectrails.htm
  Like anywhere in Colorado, the Four Corners region offers numerous hiking and biking trails. Detailed information is available at these and other websites.

- **Horseback Riding**   durango.org
  "Saddle Up!" There are numerous stables in the area offering horseback riding excursions.

- **Rafting**   see websites below
  Put on your helmet, PFD, and prepare to get wet. Numerous companies offer guided raft trips down the Animas River.

- **Skiing**   ski-hesperus.com
  During the winter months, enjoy this "locals' favorite" ski resort for downhill skiing and tubing.

- **Vallecito Lake**   vallecitolakechamber.com
  From fishing to snowshoeing to the Tour of Carvings, this beautiful lake offers numerous, year-round outdoor activities.

For further information, please visit these websites:
durango.org   cortezchamber.com   doloreschamber.com
ignaciochamber.org   bayfield.org   mancosvalley.com
co.laplata.co.us/visitors   vallecitolakechamber.com

FOUR CORNERS REGION
Additional Tasting Locations

Durango Coffee Company (Fox Fire Farms)
730 Main Avenue, Durango, CO 81301
970-259-2059
cooksandcoffee.com
Owner: Tim Wheeler
Hours: Summer, Friday and Saturday from 3 to 8 p.m.; Winter, Friday and Saturday from 2 to 7 p.m.

Honeyville Tasting Room (Meadery of the Rockies, St. Kathryn Cellars, Talon Winery)
33633 Hwy 550, Durango, CO 81301
800-676-7690
honeyvillecolorado.com
Owner: Danny and Sheree Culhane
Hours: Daily, Summer from 8 a.m. to 6 p.m.; Winter from 9 a.m. to 5 p.m.

Sutcliffe Vineyards Tasting Room (Sutcliffe Vineyards)
600 Main Avenue #102, Durango, CO 81301
970-382-0090
360durango.com
Owner: John Sutcliffe
Hours: Daily, Noon to 6 p.m.

West Fork Gallery (Sutcliffe Vineyards)
105 S. 5th Street, Dolores, CO 81323
970-882-2211
westforkgallery.com
Owner: Michelle Martin
Hours: Monday through Saturday from 7 a.m. to 5 p.m. (Event Tastings from 5 to 9 p.m.)

Front Range Region

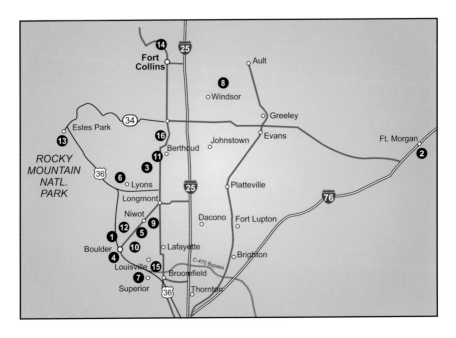

Front Range Region Wineries - North

1. Augustina's Winery
2. Bijou Creek Vineyards
3. Blue Mountain Vineyards
4. Bookcliff Vineyards
5. Boulder Creek Winery
6. Ciatano Winery
7. HoneyJack Meadery
8. Hunters Moon Meadery
9. Medovina
10. Redstone Meadery
11. St. Vrain Vineyards & Winery
12. Settembre Cellars
13. Snowy Peak Winery
14. Ten Bears Winery
15. Turquoise Mesa Winery
16. Zephyr Cellars

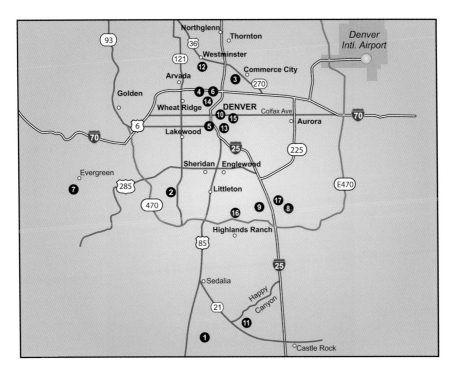

Front Range Region Wineries - South

1. Allis Ranch Winery
2. Avanti Winery
3. Balistreri Vineyards
4. Bonacquisti Wine Company
5. Colorado Cider Company
6. Colorado Winery Row
7. Creekside Cellars
8. Desert Moon Vineyards
9. Dithyramb Vineyards
10. D'Vine Wine - Home of Wild Women Wine
11. Ruby Trust Cellars
12. Spero Winery
13. The Infinite Monkey Theorem
14. Verso Cellars
15. Vino di Maria
16. Water2Wine - Centennial
17. Water2Wine - DTC

ALLIS RANCH WINERY
901 Allis Ranch Road, Sedalia, CO 80135
303-881-1294
AllisRanchWine.com
allisranchwine@gmail.com

OWNER: David Rhyne

YEAR BEGAN OPERATION: 2007

AVERAGE CASES PRODUCED ANNUALLY: 400-500

WINES PRODUCED:
White: Viognier
Red: Grenache, Reserve Syrah, Two Husky Red (Syrah)
Other: Rosé

MESSAGE FROM OWNER: Allis Ranch Winery is a family-owned, boutique winery near Sedalia, Colorado. We focus on Rhone varietals using small-lot vinification to create focused, handcrafted wines. All grapes are sourced from top growers on the Western Slope of Colorado. Allis Ranch Winery uses sustainable practices throughout the operation by minimizing the use of water and energy wherever possible.

After a great deal of research and samplings of Colorado wines, we determined that the Western Slope area offers a climate and altitude that would highlight the qualities of the grapes which originated in the Southern Rhone area of France. The hot days and cool nights bring out the classic fruit and black pepper of Syrah and the melon, floral and citric character in Viognier. Co-fermenting the Viognier grape with the Syrah, adds depth and structure to the Syrah. In 2008, we began blending Grenache and Syrah for some very unique interpretations of Colorado's own Rhone Rangers.

TASTING ROOM INFORMATION: By appointment only

DIRECTIONS: From I-25 and Exit #182 (Wilcox Wolfensberger Road in Castle Rock): Head west on Wolfensberger Road; turn left (south) onto Hwy 105 (Perry Park Road); at 1.3 miles turn right (west) onto Allis Ranch Road.

OTHER AMENITIES AT WINERY: N/A

WINE AVAILABLE FOR PURCHASE OUTSIDE OF WINERY: Yes

OTHER TASTING ROOM LOCATIONS: No

NOTES: _____

_____

_____

_____

AUGUSTINA'S WINERY
4715 N. Broadway B-3, Boulder, CO 80304
303-545-2047
winechick.biz
winechic@boulder.net

OWNER: Marianne "Gussie" Walter

YEAR BEGAN OPERATION: 1997

AVERAGE CASES PRODUCED ANNUALLY: 600

WINES PRODUCED:
White: Sauvignon Blanc
Red: Cabernet Franc, Merlot, Pinot Noir, Shiraz,
Other: Blends called Bottoms Up Red, Boulder Porch White,
WineChick White, WineChick Cherry, Venus de Vino Rosé

MESSAGE FROM OWNER: Augustina's Winery is the oldest winery in Boulder County. It is the only one-woman winery in Colorado (and possibly even the nation!). I use only Colorado-grown grapes to make wines, which go with backpacking adventures, poker parties, good books or trashy novels and gingersnaps. My wines' names reflect the variety of ways you can enjoy my delicious wines!

TASTING ROOM INFORMATION: Open Saturday afternoons (call ahead for hours). Other times by appointment only. Generally closed during February.

DIRECTIONS: From downtown Boulder: Head north on Broadway about 3.5 miles; turn left (west) at 4715 N. Broadway (by seasonal greenhouse/nursery). Behind the nursery is a warehouse building. The winery is on the south side - #B3.

OTHER AMENITIES AT WINERY: N/A

WINE AVAILABLE FOR PURCHASE OUTSIDE OF WINERY: No

OTHER TASTING ROOM LOCATIONS: No

NOTES: _____

_____

_____

_____

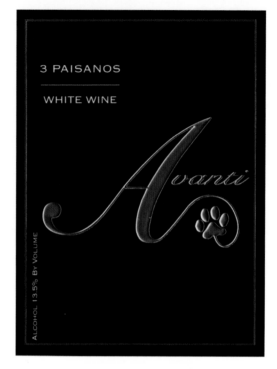

AVANTI WINERY

9046 W. Bowles Avenue, Littleton, CO 80123
303-904-7650
avantiwinery.com
grifgarman@aol.com

OWNER: Jim "Griff" Griffin

YEAR BEGAN OPERATION: 1997

AVERAGE CASES PRODUCED ANNUALLY: Information not Available

WINES PRODUCED:
White: Chardonnay
Red: Reserve Cabernet Sauvignon, Reserve Merlot
Other: Blends called 3 Paisanos White Table Wine, DueAmori,
Grassetto Rosso, Bambino Tuscano, Niko's Classico, Three Amigos,
Mystique, Port III

MESSAGE FROM OWNER: Avanti Winery was actually started as a way to promote other Colorado wineries. Currently we offer a variety of wines from over 20 different wineries. Please see our website for a complete listing. Our Avanti wines are a unique blend of the finest grapes grown. We have a sommelier on staff to assist with the blending, to insure the highest quality wines possible.

Owner "Griff" Griffin, who has lived in Colorado since 1971, and his wife, Jan, a Denver native, enjoy sharing their Colorado knowledge and can assist you in organizing your itinerary as you travel around Colorado's scenic by-ways. Stop by the winery for information as well as sampling!

TASTING ROOM INFORMATION: Thursday through Saturday from 10 a.m. to 6 p.m., Sunday from 11 a.m. to 4 p.m.

DIRECTIONS: From the intersection of Wadsworth Boulevard and Bowles Avenue in Littleton: Head west on Bowles Avenue. The winery is located on the south side of Southwest Plaza, between Guirys and Carpet Mill.

OTHER AMENITIES AT WINERY: A walk-in humidor featuring all major cigar brands (non-smoking facility)

WINE AVAILABLE FOR PURCHASE OUTSIDE OF WINERY: Yes

OTHER TASTING ROOM LOCATIONS: No

NOTES: _____

_____

_____

_____

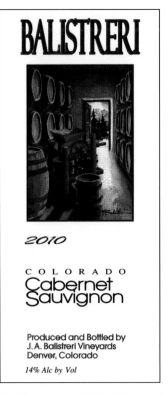

BALISTRERI VINEYARDS

1946 E. 66th Avenue, Denver, CO 80229
303-287-5156
balistrerivineyards.com
info@balistreriwine.com

OWNER: John, Birdie and Julie Balistreri

YEAR BEGAN OPERATION: 1998

AVERAGE CASES PRODUCED ANNUALLY: 5,000

WINES PRODUCED:
White: Chardonnay, dry Muscat, Viognier
Red: Cabernet Franc, Cabernet Sauvignon, Merlot, Petit Sirah,
Sangiovese, Syrah, Tempranillo, Zinfandel
Other: Dessert wines

MESSAGE FROM OWNER: Balistreri Vineyards is a family-owned and operated winery dedicated to making fine-quality wine. John Balistreri's wines are made completely natural, with a very approachable, easy-drinking style. He combines both traditional winemaking methods and modern technology to produce award-winning wines. The wines are handcrafted one barrel at a time, with grapes that are fermented on their own yeast, unaltered by sulfates, unfiltered, unfined and aged in American oak.

TASTING ROOM INFORMATION: Daily, from noon to 5 p.m.

DIRECTIONS: From the intersection of I-25 and 58th Avenue: Head east on 58th Avenue; turn left (north) onto York Street; turn left (west) onto 66th Street. Also accessible off I-270 and York Street exit.

OTHER AMENITIES AT WINERY: Wine-related gifts, antipasti items and wine gift baskets. During the summer months you can order antipasti from our patio menu during business hours. The Winery is also available for private parties and events after hours.

WINE AVAILABLE FOR PURCHASE OUTSIDE OF WINERY: Yes

OTHER TASTING ROOM LOCATIONS: No

NOTES: _____

_____

_____

_____

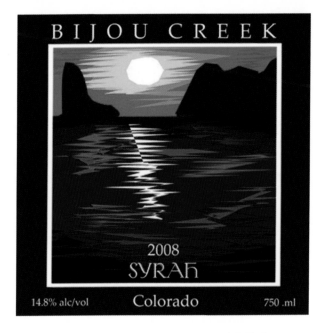

BIJOU CREEK VINEYARDS

18969 County Road 11, Fort Morgan, CO 80701

970-542-9538

bijoucreekwine.com

ewhillmann@earthlink.net

OWNER: Erwin Hillmann

YEAR BEGAN OPERATION: 2006

AVERAGE CASES PRODUCED ANNUALLY: 300

WINES PRODUCED:
White: Chardonnay, Riesling
Red: Cabernet Franc, Merlot, Syrah
Other: None

MESSAGE FROM OWNER: Our wine is made by time-tested traditions handed down for generations, complemented by modern technology. That combination makes our wines as good as can be made from premium, high-altitude Colorado grapes. Hot days and cool nights combined with intense sunlight make these grapes rich in color and flavor, with just the right balance of acid and tannins.

Located in Eastern Colorado, near Fort Morgan, Bijou Creek Winery is named after the seasonally dry creek that meanders through the region, which was named by early French explorers. We currently receive our grapes from the Western Slope, but here at our winery, we are experimenting with grapes that make good wine, more suited to Eastern Colorado. We currently do not have a tasting room available but will soon be relocating to our new winery building, which will be open for wine tasting and other events.

TASTING ROOM INFORMATION: Coming soon

DIRECTIONS: N/A

OTHER AMENITIES AT WINERY: N/A

WINE AVAILABLE FOR PURCHASE OUTSIDE OF WINERY: Yes

OTHER TASTING ROOM LOCATIONS: Highlands Ranch Farmers Market

NOTES: _____

_____

_____

_____

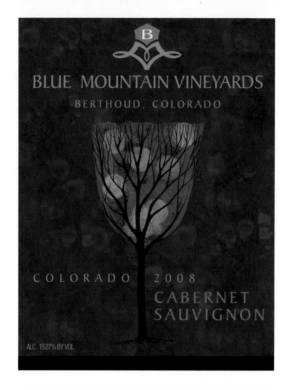

BLUE MOUNTAIN VINEYARDS

4480 Hoot Owl Drive, Berthoud, CO 80513
303-772-8942
coloradobluemountain.com
bill@coloradobluemountain.com

OWNER: Bill Prewitt

YEAR BEGAN OPERATION: 2007

AVERAGE CASES PRODUCED ANNUALLY: Information not Available

WINES PRODUCED:
White: Chardonnay, Gewürztraminer, Pinot Grigio, Riesling, Sauvignon Blanc
Red: Cabernet Sauvignon, Merlot, Pinot Noir, Sangiovese, Zinfandel
Other: None

MESSAGE FROM OWNER: Our vineyard, winery and grounds are all built on the edge of a lake, with breathtaking scenery. Owner, Bill Prewitt has been making wine for over 42 years. Our vineyard and winery are family owned, like most in Colorado, and we want to make a nice wine that our customers can depend on for quality. Our wines are deep and rich for the reds, and wonderful and fruity for the whites. Sangiovese is our best seller three to one! We really encourage all of our customers to taste our wines before they buy them, to make sure they meet their taste profile. If you cannot travel to our Tasting Room, the wines are also available at liquor stores in Denver, Estes Park, Fort Collins, Greeley, Longmont and Loveland.

TASTING ROOM INFORMATION: By appointment only

DIRECTIONS: Directions will be provided at time of tasting appointment confirmation.

OTHER AMENITIES AT WINERY: Beautiful gardens behind our Winery with a deck overlooking the lake with Rocky Mountain National Park and Indian Peaks Wilderness as the backdrop.

WINE AVAILABLE FOR PURCHASE OUTSIDE OF WINERY: Yes

OTHER TASTING ROOM LOCATIONS: Farmers Markets in Estes Park and Fort Collins-County Extension and Opera Galleria, a winter market in downtown Fort Collins.

NOTES: _____

_____

_____

_____

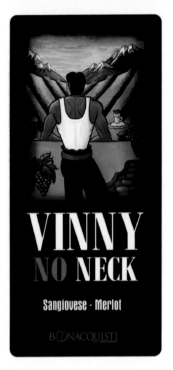

BONACQUISTI WINE COMPANY

4640 Pecos Street, Unit I, Denver CO 80211
303-477-9463
denverwine.net
paul@denverwine.net

OWNER: Paul and Judi Bonacquisti

YEAR BEGAN OPERATION: 2006

AVERAGE CASES PRODUCED ANNUALLY: 1,500

WINES PRODUCED:
White: Pinot Grigio, Riesling
Red: Cabernet Franc, Cabernet Sauvignon, Sangiovese, Syrah, Zinfandel
Other: Blends called [d] Red, Vinny No Neck and Bella Risa; Port wine

MESSAGE FROM OWNER: Bonacquisti Wine Company opened its doors in October 2006, introducing Denver's Urban Winery to Colorado. Winemaker and Executive Sommelier Paul Bonacquisti is a second generation Italian-American, who learned to make wine from his dad, who learned to make wine from his dad. Bonacquisti creates award-winning wines in various styles: easy drinking, every-night-of-the-week blends and our reserve and limited production varietal wines that are also enjoyable every night of the week.

As a Denver company located in the Sunnyside neighborhood at I-70 and Pecos, Bonacquisti Wine Company supports local education and local art. The winery is a family affair with perennial favorites, Vinny No Neck and Bella Risa, named for our children. If you stop at the retail sales room of the winery during the week, you will likely be greeted by our dog, Koda.

TASTING ROOM INFORMATION: Thursday through Saturday from 11 a.m. to 5 p.m.

DIRECTIONS: From the intersection of I-70 and Exit #273 (Pecos Street): Head south on Pecos Street; turn left (east) into Colorado Winery Row's parking lot (by Quiznos), which is just north of 46th Avenue.

OTHER AMENITIES AT WINERY: The Winery is available to rent for gatherings up to 100 people.

WINE AVAILABLE FOR PURCHASE OUTSIDE OF WINERY: Yes

OTHER TASTING ROOM LOCATIONS: No

NOTES: _____

_____

_____

_____

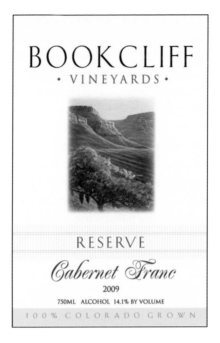

BOOKCLIFF VINEYARDS

1501 Lee Hill Road, Road #17, Boulder, CO 80304
303-449-9463
bookcliffvineyards.com
winery@bookcliffvineyards.com

OWNER: John Garlich and Ulla Merz

YEAR BEGAN OPERATION: 1999

AVERAGE CASES PRODUCED ANNUALLY: 3,300

WINES PRODUCED:
White: Chardonnay, Riesling, Viognier
Red: Cabernet Franc, Cabernet Sauvignon, Petite Sirah, Syrah, Tempranillo
Other: Blends called A Touch of Red, Ensemble, Friday's Folly, Lucky Twenty and several others

MESSAGE FROM OWNER: Bookcliff Vineyards is a Boulder, Colorado, winery making award-winning wines. Our wines are made from 100% Colorado-grown grapes, from our vineyards in Palisade. We own and operate 26 acres of vineyards growing 12 different varieties of grapes, using sustainable farming practices.

John and Ulla, the owners, are both engineers by profession and planted the first six acres of grape vines in 1996, and licensed the winery in 1999. We strive to make wines that are true to the varietal character of the grapes, without adding any color or flavor enhancers. Premier offerings include Ensemble, a Bordeaux-style blend, Cabernet Franc and Petite Sirah. We regularly host local chefs, offering wine- and food-pairing dinners at the winery. Come join us!

TASTING ROOM INFORMATION: January through May, Friday through Sunday from 1 to 6 p.m.; June through December, Thursday through Sunday from 1 to 6 p.m

DIRECTIONS: From downtown Boulder: Drive north on Broadway; turn right (east) onto Lee Hill Drive (changes to Road). Lee Hill Road is the last intersection before Broadway and 28th Street merge.

OTHER AMENITIES AT WINERY: Wine-related merchandise for sale and rental space is available for sit-down dinners (up to 36 people) and meeting space (up to 50 people).

WINE AVAILABLE FOR PURCHASE OUTSIDE OF WINERY: Yes

OTHER TASTING ROOM LOCATIONS: The Chocolate Moose and Ice Cream Parlor (see Mountain Region)

NOTES: _____

_____

_____

_____

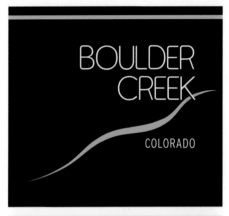

BOULDER CREEK WINERY

6440 Odell Place, Boulder, CO 80301
303-516-9031
bouldercreekwine.com
info@bouldercreekwine.com

OWNER: Jackie and Mike Thompson

YEAR BEGAN OPERATION: 2003

AVERAGE CASES PRODUCED ANNUALLY: 2,000

WINES PRODUCED:
White: Chardonnay, Riesling, Viognier, White Merlot
Red: Cabernet Franc, Cabernet Sauvignon, Merlot, Syrah
Other: Blends called Consensus and Murphy's Choice, Dry Rosé,
Zinfandel Port

MESSAGE FROM OWNER: Founded in 2003 by owner and winemaker Jackie Thompson, Boulder Creek Winery makes "serious" award-winning wines from Colorado grapes. Stop in and see for yourselves. We will exceed your expectations!

TASTING ROOM INFORMATION: Thursday through Sunday from 1 to 5:30 p.m.

DIRECTIONS: From the intersection of Hwy 119 (Longmont Diagonal) and 63rd Street in Boulder: Head south on 63rd Street; turn left (east) onto Lookout Road; turn left (north) onto Spine Road; turn left (west) onto Odell Place.

OTHER AMENITIES AT WINERY: Self-guided Winery tour and gift shop

WINE AVAILABLE FOR PURCHASE OUTSIDE OF WINERY: Yes

OTHER TASTING ROOM LOCATIONS: No

NOTES: _____

_____

_____

_____

CIATANO WINERY
16858 N. St. Vrain Drive, Lyons, CO 80540
303-823-5011
ciatanowinery.com
wine@ciatanowinery.com

OWNER: The Gibson Family

YEAR BEGAN OPERATION: 1998

AVERAGE CASES PRODUCED ANNUALLY: 1,000

WINES PRODUCED:
White: Riesling, Viognier, White Merlot
Red: Cabernet Franc, Cabernet Sauvignon, Pinot Noir, Sangiovese, Syrah
Other: Blends called Bianco Cambiani and Cambiani Rosso

MESSAGE FROM OWNER: We offer a unique Colorado experience, where you can stay at our family-owned winery, enjoy premium Colorado wines made onsite at Ciatano Winery and indulge the senses at our day spa, La Bellezza. The Rock N' River is just minutes from Rocky Mountain National Park and Estes Park.

TASTING ROOM INFORMATION: Memorial Day weekend through October, daily, from 11 a.m. to 7 p.m.; November through April, Friday through Monday from 11 a.m. to 5 p.m.

DIRECTIONS: From downtown Lyons (Hwy 7/Hwy 36/Hwy 66): Head north on Hwy 36/66 towards Estes Park. The winery is a few miles outside of town.

OTHER AMENITIES AT WINERY: Rock N' River Day Resort featuring La Bellezza Spa, as well as lodging, specializing in weddings, retreats and reunions.

WINE AVAILABLE FOR PURCHASE OUTSIDE OF WINERY: Yes

OTHER TASTING ROOM LOCATIONS: No

NOTES: _____

_____

_____

_____

Alc. 6.95% by vol | 650 ml | CONTAINS SULFITES | GLUTEN FREE PURE CRAFT CIDER

COLORADO CIDER COMPANY

2650 W. 2nd Avenue #10, Denver, CO 80219

303-759-3560

coloradocider.com

info@coloradocider.com

OWNER: Colorado Cider Company LLC

YEAR BEGAN OPERATION: 2010

AVERAGE CASES PRODUCED ANNUALLY: 1,500

WINES PRODUCED:

White: None

Red: None

Other: Glider Cider, Glider Cider Dry, Grasshop-ah Cider and Ol' Stumpy Cider

MESSAGE FROM OWNER: Colorado Cider Company is a craft Cidery dedicated to making all juice ciders, with as much Colorado apples as possible. We make Dry Ciders and showcase the apple flavor over sweetness. The owners are developing an orchard outside Hotchkiss and plan on growing traditional cider apple varieties in the future.

TASTING ROOM INFORMATION: Friday from 3 to 6 p.m., Saturday from 2:30 to 6:30 p.m. Other times by appointment only (this is a production facility).

DIRECTIONS: From the intersection of I-25 and Sixth Avenue: Head west on Sixth Avenue; exit at Bryant Street; turn left (south) onto Bryant Street; turn right (west) onto 2nd Avenue; turn left into 2650 W. 2nd Avenue. We are the last warehouse south - #10.

OTHER AMENITIES AT WINERY: N/A

WINE AVAILABLE FOR PURCHASE OUTSIDE OF WINERY: Yes

OTHER TASTING ROOM LOCATIONS: No

NOTES: _____

_____

_____

_____

COLORADO WINERY ROW

4640 Pecos Street, Denver, CO 80211
coloradowineryrow.com

Bonacquisti Wine Company: 303-477-9463
denverwine.net
Cottonwood Cellars & The Olathe Winery: 720-855-6500
cottonwoodcellars.com
Garfield Estates Vineyard & Winery: 303-455-2200
garfieldestates.com
Verso Cellars: 303-587-9740
versocellars.com

OWNER: Bonacquisti Wine Company, Cottonwood Cellars, Garfield Estates Vineyard & Winery and Verso Cellars

YEAR BEGAN OPERATION: 2010

AVERAGE CASES PRODUCED ANNUALLY: N/A

WINES PRODUCED:
See individual winery websites for more information.

MESSAGE FROM OWNER: Our four celebrated artisan Colorado wineries are known for producing award-winning wines, including Chardonnay, Riesling, Cabernet Sauvignon, Syrah and other varietal wine. Denver's Urban Wine Tasting Destination™ is conveniently located off of I-70 and Pecos, in the Highlands, just minutes away from LODO and Downtown Denver.

While most of Colorado's grapes are grown on the Western Slope, four hours west of Denver, Colorado Winery Row provides a unique opportunity to taste boutique wines, with proprietors and winemakers. Best of all, you don't have to be a wine geek to gain access to the wine world. Wine tasting without the attitude is our specialty! Come and enjoy local wines in a relaxed, urban setting, with knowledgeable and entertaining hosts, eager to share their passion for wine.

TASTING ROOM INFORMATION: Thursday through Saturday from noon to 5 p.m.; Available for private wine tastings by appointment.

DIRECTIONS: From I-70 and Exit #273 (Pecos Street): Head south on Pecos Street; turn left (east) into Colorado Winery Row parking lot by Quiznos, which is just before 46th Avenue.

OTHER AMENITIES AT WINERY: Local art/mixed media pieces are exhibited throughout; enjoy monthly "Uncorked" events with live music, wines by the glass and select food pairings; Colorado Winery Row is available for private events and wine tasting.

WINE AVAILABLE FOR PURCHASE OUTSIDE OF WINERY: Yes

OTHER TASTING ROOM LOCATIONS: See individual winery websites for more information.

NOTES: _____

_____

_____

_____

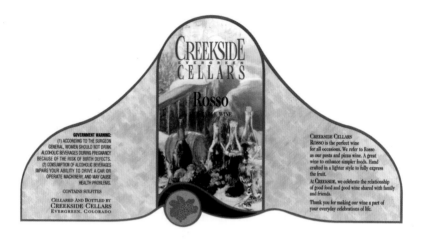

CREEKSIDE CELLARS

28036 Hwy 74, Evergreen, CO 80439

303-674-5460

creeksidecellars.net

info@creeksidecellars.net

OWNER: Bill and Anita Donahue

YEAR BEGAN OPERATION: 1996

AVERAGE CASES PRODUCED ANNUALLY: 3,000

WINES PRODUCED:

White: Chardonnay, Gewürztraminer, Riesling, Viognier

Red: Cabernet Franc, Cabernet Sauvignon, Merlot, Petit Sirah, Petit Verdot, Syrah,

Other: Blends called Bianco and Rosso; various Port wines

MESSAGE FROM OWNER: Our wines are handcrafted from grapes grown in the Grand Valley AVA of Colorado's Western Slope. All of our wines are produced and bottled at our Evergreen location. At Creekside Cellars, we celebrate the relationship of good food and good wine, shared with family and friends.

Creekside Cellars features a full-service restaurant along with our winery, which overlooks Bear Creek. Stop by for one of our famous antipasto platters and a bottle of wine after snowshoeing, ice skating, hiking or mountain biking!

TASTING ROOM INFORMATION: Daily, from 11 a.m. to 5 p.m.

DIRECTIONS: From the intersection of I-70 and Exit #252 (westbound) #251 (eastbound) at the Evergreen/El Rancho exit: Head south on Evergreen Parkway/Hwy 74 approximately 8 miles into town. The winery is on your right (south) side.

OTHER AMENITIES AT WINERY: A café along the banks of Bear Creek; monthly wine pairing dinners; "New Release" parties; available to rent for various events accommodating up to 50 people; catering service.

WINE AVAILABLE FOR PURCHASE OUTSIDE OF WINERY: Yes

OTHER TASTING ROOM LOCATIONS: No

NOTES: _____

_____

_____

_____

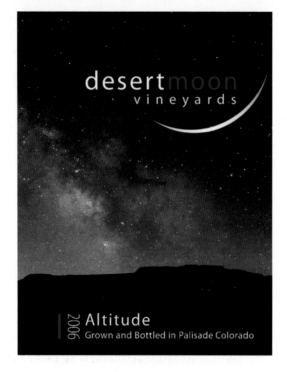

DESERT MOON VINEYARDS
12656 E. Jamison Place #12, Englewood, CO 80112
303-990-9463
desertmoonvineyards.com
info@desertmoonvineyards.com

OWNER: Debra Ray

YEAR BEGAN OPERATION: 2005

AVERAGE CASES PRODUCED ANNUALLY: Information not Available

WINES PRODUCED:
White: Pinot Grigio, Riesling
Red: Merlot
Other: Blend called Altitude, Port wine, Shiver (an ice-style)

MESSAGE FROM OWNER: Desert Moon Vineyards began in 2002 when we purchased a 20-acre farm in Palisade. We planted our favorite grapes – Cabernet Sauvignon, Merlot and a little Syrah - and, in 2004, produced our first vintage of 50 cases.

In 2010, we moved our winemaking to the Denver Tech Center and opened our first tasting room. We are excited to make wine in the highest altitude, and perhaps, most unforgiving climate in the United States. We believe the sun, soil and climate combine to produce wines of intense character. Stop in for a taste!

TASTING ROOM INFORMATION: Saturday and Sunday from 1 to 5 p.m.

DIRECTIONS: From I-25 and Exit #197 (Arapahoe Road): Head east on Arapahoe Road; turn right (south) onto Peoria Street (which changes to Broncos Parkway); turn right (south) onto Adam Aircraft Circle; turn right (west) onto Jamison Place. Winery is on the left.

OTHER AMENITIES AT WINERY: Old-World-style Barrel Room for classes and events.

WINE AVAILABLE FOR PURCHASE OUTSIDE OF WINERY: Yes

OTHER TASTING ROOM LOCATIONS: No

NOTES: _____

_____

_____

_____

CABERNET SAUVIGNON
2009

Alc.
15.0% by
Vol.

DITHYRAMB

GRAND
VALLEY
AVA

DITHYRAMB WINERY

8312 E. Briarwood Boulevard, Centennial, CO 80112
720-529-3846
dithyrambwinery.com
info@dithyrambwinery.com

OWNER: Sean and Candice Bundy

YEAR BEGAN OPERATION: 2008

AVERAGE CASES PRODUCED ANNUALLY: 500

WINES PRODUCED:
White: Orange Muscat, Riesling, Sauvignon Blanc
Red: Cabernet Franc, Cabernet Sauvignon, Merlot, Syrah
Other: Red Blends; various Meads and Honey wine

MESSAGE FROM OWNER: Sean and Candice Bundy began making wine and mead when they were married in 1995 after their friends gifted them with a homebrew set as a wedding gift. (So you can either thank them, or rue their gift choice!) Over the years, the Bundys' love of wine and mead and all things brewed, grew and grew. They dreamed of a day when their brewing would become more than a hobby. In 2008, Sean wrote to the city of Centennial asking for approval to start a home-based winery, and the adventure started! That summer was spent on home remodeling, paperwork and securing contracts for grapes grown on the Western Slope. Also in 2008, Sean and Candice were certified as Executive Wine Sommeliers.

All of the wines and meads produced at Dithyramb Winery are done in small, hand-crafted batches and receive oodles of personalized attention. The name Dithyramb is a hymn sung to Dionysos, the Greek God of Wine.

TASTING ROOM INFORMATION: By appointment only

DIRECTIONS: Given at time of appointment.

OTHER AMENITIES AT WINERY: N/A

WINE AVAILABLE FOR PURCHASE OUTSIDE OF WINERY: Yes

OTHER TASTING ROOM LOCATIONS: Mountain Rains Gallery and Gifts (see Pikes Peak Region)

NOTES: _____

_____

_____

_____

D'VINE WINE
Home of WILD WOMEN WINE
1660 Champa Street, Denver, CO 80202
303-534-0788
winerydenver.com
winery@winerydenver.com

OWNER: Charlene and Ross Meriwether

YEAR BEGAN OPERATION: 2007

AVERAGE CASES PRODUCED ANNUALLY: 3,000

WINES PRODUCED:
White: Naked Chardonnay, Peach Chardonnay, Pinot Grigio,
Green Apple Riesling, Sauvignon Blanc
Red: Blackberry Merlot, Nebiolo, Pinot Noir, Raspberry Noir,
Tempranillo
Other: Several red blends, Grapefruit Blush, Chocolate Port

MESSAGE FROM OWNER: Wild Women Wine is a brand of D'Vine Wine, a boutique winery franchise that sources juice from California vineyards. Ross, the vintner, and his wife, Charlene, aka Chief Wild Woman, bring you 17 varietals ranging from a Naked Chardonnay to unusual blends such as the Hot Stiletto, a Zinfandel/Syrah blend. They include favorites such as Tempranillo and Nebiolo, and finish with their signature Royal Ruby, a chocolate port.

Each wine features its own entertaining label from the artwork of Jill Neal. Their compact winery operation and warm, inviting tasting room are found in the middle of downtown Denver, and offer tastings, wine by the glass, or wine by the bottle in a relaxing, fun atmosphere. Their motto: "If you're not having fun, we'll ask you to leave!"

TASTING ROOM INFORMATION: Tuesday through Sunday from noon to 8 p.m.

DIRECTIONS: From I-25 and Exit #210B (Auraria Parkway): Head northeast on Auraria Parkway; turn right (south) onto Speer Boulevard; turn left (northeast) onto Lawrence Street; turn right (south) onto 17th Street; turn right (southwest) onto Champa Street. Winery is on the left (north) side.

OTHER AMENITIES AT WINERY: Wine-related merchandise, personalized wine labels on any varietal, wine tasting parties, wine bottling parties

WINE AVAILABLE FOR PURCHASE OUTSIDE OF WINERY: Yes

OTHER TASTING ROOM LOCATIONS: D'Vine Wine-Breckenridge (see Mountain Region)

NOTES: _____

_____

_____

_____

HONEYJACK MEADERY

9769 W. 119th Drive, Bay 7, Broomfield, CO 80021
Dan: 303-746-0193
Jimmy: 303-709-7422
honeyjack.com
Dan@honeyjack.com
Jimmy@honeyjack.com

OWNER: Dan Bowron and Jimmy Bowron

YEAR BEGAN OPERATION: 2009

AVERAGE CASES PRODUCED ANNUALLY: Information not Available

WINES PRODUCED:
White: None
Red: None
Other: Mead

MESSAGE FROM OWNER: HoneyJack Meadery was started by Dan Bowron, as he enjoyed home winemaking for years. After a decade of perfecting his recipe, he launched HoneyJack Meadery so the public could enjoy his honey wine.

   Our mead is 100% all natural, handmade honey wine. Made with fresh organic fruits, we never add sulfites, acids or chemicals of any kind to aid in the fermentation process. We ferment and age naturally in brand-new, toasted oak barrels to give that perfect Old World mead flavor.

TASTING ROOM INFORMATION: By appointment only

DIRECTIONS: From I-25 and Hwy 36 (the Boulder Turnpike): Head west towards Boulder; exit at #121/Wadsworth Boulevard; head south on Wadsworth Boulevard; turn right (west) onto Metro Airport Avenue; turn right (north) onto 119th Drive. The Meadery is located on the west side of the building.

OTHER AMENITIES AT WINERY: We are very small, but can host parties in the summer for up to 100 people.

WINE AVAILABLE FOR PURCHASE OUTSIDE OF WINERY: Yes

OTHER TASTING ROOM LOCATIONS: No

NOTES: _____

_____

_____

_____

RENAISSANCE: noun - a renewal of life, vigor, interest; rebirth; revival

WELCOME TO THE RENAISSANCE OF MEAD

Mead, also referred to as Honey Wine is believed to be the oldest known alcoholic beverage. In recent years it has begun to regain its place in history. We are a small family owned Colorado meadery. We brew in small batches to ensure quality control and we harvest honey from our own bees. We use the best ingredients available and taste frequently! The meads we create are great for any event, whether a small picnic, a fancy wedding, tailgate party or just sitting on the front porch watching the stars. So, remember to BRING ALONG THE MOON™

PRODUCED AND BOTTLED BY TWO BEES LLC SEVERANCE, COLORADO U.S.A.
www.huntersmoonmeadery.com

Artwork by: kelly apgar

HUNTERS MOON MEADERY

THIS MEAD IS MADE WITH COLORADO WILDFLOWER HONEY. OUR BEEHIVES ARE PLACED NEAR A VARIETY OF NECTAR SOURCES WHICH CREATES UNIQUE FLAVORS. WE RECOMMEND SERVING LIGHTLY CHILLED. ENJOY RESPONSIBLY, GREG & KIM

NO SULFITES ADDED NATURALLY OCCURRING SULFITES MAY EXIST.

GOVERNMENT WARNING: (1) ACCORDING TO THE SURGEON GENERAL, WOMEN SHOULD NOT DRINK ALCOHOLIC BEVERAGES DURING PREGNANCY BECAUSE OF THE RISK OF BIRTH DEFECTS. (2) CONSUMPTION OF ALCOHOLIC BEVERAGES IMPAIRS YOUR ABILITY TO DRIVE A CAR OR OPERATE MACHINERY, AND MAY CAUSE HEALTH PROBLEMS.

TWO BEES MEAD
SEMI-SWEET HONEY WINE
ALCOHOL BY VOLUME 12%   750ML   GLUTEN FREE

HUNTERS MOON MEADERY
404 Immigrant Trail, Severance, CO 80550
970-686-6706
huntersmoonmeadery.com
kim@huntersmoonmeadery.com

OWNER: Greg and Kim Bowdish

YEAR BEGAN OPERATION: 2010

AVERAGE CASES PRODUCED ANNUALLY: 110 first year, Project 300 in 2012

WINES PRODUCED:
White: None
Red: None
Other: Meads called Semi-Sweet Kim's Clove Metheglin, Semi-Sweet Lunar Lemon Melomel, Mountain and Trappers Cask

MESSAGE FROM OWNER: We are a new, family-owned Meadery/ Honey Winery on the North Front Range of Colorado. We started production in December, 2010. We do not rush our meads, which take eight to twelve months to mature before bottling. The majority of our meads are semi-sweet, although we have some that are off-dry and sweet as well. We do not use grapes in our Mead/Honey Wine, but use the honey from our 40 bee hives. Our Mead production is limited by the amount of honey that our own honeybees bring in each year.

TASTING ROOM INFORMATION: By appointment only

DIRECTIONS: Please call for directions, as our facility is in a residential area.

OTHER AMENITIES AT WINERY: N/A

WINE AVAILABLE FOR PURCHASE OUTSIDE OF WINERY: Yes

OTHER TASTING ROOM LOCATIONS: No

NOTES: _____

_____

_____

_____

MEDOVINA
308 Third Avenue, Niwot, CO 80544
303-845-3090
medovina.com
mark@medovina.com

OWNER: Mark and Kellie Beran

YEAR BEGAN OPERATION: Information not Available

AVERAGE CASES PRODUCED ANNUALLY: Information not Available

WINES PRODUCED:
White: None
Red: None
Other: Meads - Dry, Off-Dry, Semi-Sweet and Dessert; Hard Cider

MESSAGE FROM OWNER: Medovina brings you artisan Colorado Honey Wine, produced by our meadmaster, Mark Beran, and his dedicated work force of Buckfast bees, now over half a million strong. Medovina produces its own honey, from which it handcrafts its mead. Our beeyards are nestled in Old Town Niwot – in the shade of large cottonwoods planted nearly a century ago by early homesteaders.

As summer gives way to autumn, Medovina begins harvesting the honey and crafting its mead. Our Old World process preserves the rich floral extracts present in our honey. Our meads are produced naturally, without filtering or added sulfites. Alcohol, honey and acidity are harmonized by producing our meads slowly, in small batches, and barrel aging them before bottling. Further aging occurs naturally in the bottle and full maturity can be expected in three to eight years, but you do not have to wait that long to enjoy them. Drink Mead, save a honey bee!

TASTING ROOM INFORMATION: By appointment only

DIRECTIONS: From Hwy 119 and Hwy 52 (Mineral Road): Head northeast on Hwy 119; turn right (east) onto Niwot Road; turn left (northwest) onto 2nd Avenue; turn right (northeast) onto Franklin Street; turn right (southeast) onto 3rd Avenue.

OTHER AMENITIES AT WINERY: Private tasting seminars

WINE AVAILABLE FOR PURCHASE OUTSIDE OF WINERY: Yes

OTHER TASTING ROOM LOCATIONS: No

NOTES: _____

_____

_____

_____

REDSTONE MEADERY

4700 Pearl Street, Boulder, CO 80301

720-406-1215

redstonemeadery.com

info@redstonemeadery.com

OWNER: David Myers

YEAR BEGAN OPERATION: 2000

AVERAGE CASES PRODUCED ANNUALLY: 60,000 liters
(we bottle and keg our meads)

WINES PRODUCED:
White: None
Red: None
Other: Mead - Nectars, Mountain Honey wines
and Reserve Dessert Meads

MESSAGE FROM OWNER: David Myers, known as "Chairman of the Mead," founder of Redstone Meadery, is a romantic and wants to see mead once again enjoying the glory days of yesteryear. He started the Boulder, Colorado company with the "natural philosophy" that he produce the highest quality honey wine on the market. Because of this "philosophy of mead," Redstone does not cork, but instead uses swing top bottles. In keeping with the "natural" approach, Redstone does not add any sulfites, uses only all natural ingredients and is 100% gluten-free.

Redstone only pasteurizes the must (unfermented mead) and never boils. Redstone specializes in medium to dry style meads and offers complimentary tastings of many of their award-winning meads. Remember to...Ask for Mead!

TASTING ROOM INFORMATION: Monday through Friday from noon to 6:30 p.m., Saturday from noon to 5 p.m.

DIRECTIONS: From the intersection of Hwy 36 (Boulder Turnpike) and Foothills Parkway: Head north on Foothills Parkway; take the Pearl Street exit; turn right onto Pearl Parkway at the bottom of the ramp; take an immediate left onto 47th Street; turn right (east) onto Pearl Street. The Meadery is on the right (south) side of the street.

OTHER AMENITIES AT WINERY: Winery tours (1 & 3 p.m. weekdays, 12:30 p.m. Saturdays); Mead-related merchandise; Saturday afternoon live music from 2 to 5 p.m. from November through April (free).

WINE AVAILABLE FOR PURCHASE OUTSIDE OF WINERY: Yes

OTHER TASTING ROOM LOCATIONS: No

NOTES: _____

_____

_____

_____

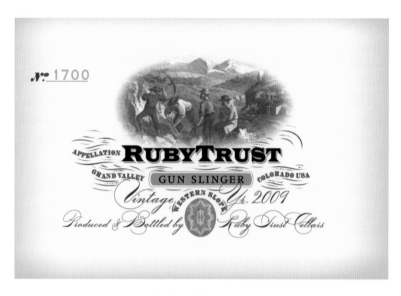

RUBY TRUST CELLARS

864 W. Happy Canyon Road #120, Castle Rock, CO 80108
720-202-2041
rubytrustcellars.com
info@rubytrustcellars.com

OWNER: Ray and Jean Bruening

YEAR BEGAN OPERATION: 2009

AVERAGE CASES PRODUCED ANNUALLY: 400 - 500

WINES PRODUCED:
White: None
Red: None
Other: Blends called Gun Slinger, The Smuggler, Fortune Seeker,
Bandit's Pass

MESSAGE FROM OWNER: Founded in 2009, Ruby Trust Cellars is a boutique winery located in picturesque Castle Rock, Colorado. We are focusing on small production, hand-crafted Colorado red wine blends.

TASTING ROOM INFORMATION: By appointment only

DIRECTIONS: From I-25 at Exit #187: Head southwest on Happy Canyon Road; just before Hwy 85, turn left (south) into the Village at Castle Pines shops. We are located behind the shops at #120.

OTHER AMENITIES AT WINERY: N/A

WINE AVAILABLE FOR PURCHASE OUTSIDE OF WINERY: Yes

OTHER TASTING ROOM LOCATIONS: No

NOTES: _____

_____

_____

_____

ST. VRAIN VINEYARDS AND WINERY

1633 S. Hwy 287, Berthoud, CO 80513
303-929-2958
Website: N/A
jayemmons@msn.com

OWNER: Roy Emmons

YEAR BEGAN OPERATION: 2003

AVERAGE CASES PRODUCED ANNUALLY: 200

WINES PRODUCED:
White: Chardonnay
Red: Merlot
Other: Blends called Little River Red, St. Vrain Reserve Red, Roy's Red, Cathy's White, Twinkle Twinkle and Plum wine

MESSAGE FROM OWNER: Owner, Roy Emmons, is a former brewmaster, who started the winery in 1998. He grows his own cold-hardy, French hybrid grapes for his wine production, obtaining additional grapes from a number of sources. Taste our delicious blends at the winery or the Longmont Farmers Market.

TASTING ROOM INFORMATION: By appointment only

DIRECTIONS: From I-25 at Exit #243 (Hwy 66): Head west on Hwy 66; turn right (north) onto Hwy 287; winery is 5 miles north on right (east) side.

OTHER AMENITIES AT WINERY: Events for small parties

WINE AVAILABLE FOR PURCHASE OUTSIDE OF WINERY: Yes

OTHER TASTING ROOM LOCATIONS: No

NOTES: _____

_____

_____

_____

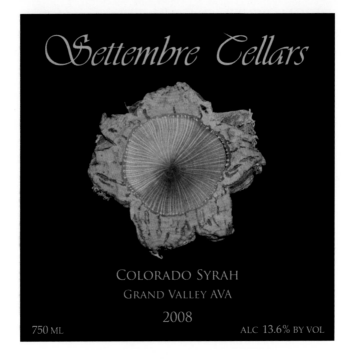

SETTEMBRE CELLARS
1780 Grape Avenue, Boulder, CO 80304
303-818-9324
SettembreCellars.com
contact@SettembreCellars.com

OWNER: Blake and Tracy Eliasson

YEAR BEGAN OPERATION: 2007

AVERAGE CASES PRODUCED ANNUALLY: 420

WINES PRODUCED:
White: Chardonnay, Riesling
Red: Cabernet Sauvignon, Sangiovese, Syrah
Other: 80304, a wine grown and produced in Boulder

MESSAGE FROM OWNER: Settembre Cellars handcrafts limited edition Colorado wines with meticulous attention to detail, that preserve the terroir of Colorado's high altitude vineyards. With a Ph.D. in Electrical Engineering and a Certificate in Enology and Viticulture from the University of California at Davis, Blake emphasizes measurement science to minimize the need for manipulation, and enables the production of exquisite wines using traditional techniques. Committed to using 100% Colorado grapes, we strive to craft world-class wines of uncompromising quality.

Inspired by the earthy elegance exhibited by wines from the Old World, our winemaking goals include balance, food friendliness and extraordinary finish. Stainless steel fermentation, moderate alcohol levels and restrained use of hand-selected French oak barrels combine to allow Colorado's high-altitude terroir to shine. With fewer than 500 cases produced each year, we truly are a small family winery.

TASTING ROOM INFORMATION: Opening soon, check website for details.

DIRECTIONS: N/A

OTHER AMENITIES AT WINERY: N/A

WINE AVAILABLE FOR PURCHASE OUTSIDE OF WINERY: Yes

OTHER TASTING ROOM LOCATIONS: No

NOTES: _____

_____

_____

_____

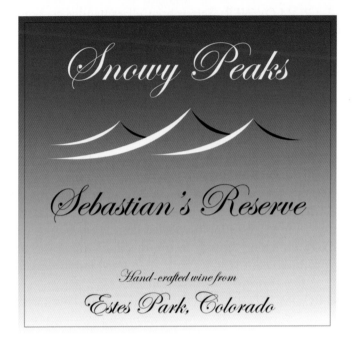

SNOWY PEAKS WINERY

292 Moraine Avenue, Estes Park, CO 80517
970-586-2099
snowypeakswinery.com
info@snowypeakswinery.com

OWNER: Erik and Candice Mohr

YEAR BEGAN OPERATION: 2005

AVERAGE CASES PRODUCED ANNUALLY: 1,200

WINES PRODUCED:
White: Riesling, Rousanne, Viognier
Red: Cabernet Franc, Cabernet Sauvignon, Cinsault, Merlot, Mourvèdre Petite Sirah, Syrah
Other: Several white and red blends, Rosé, Dessert wines

MESSAGE FROM OWNER: Taking inspiration from a business partner, Erik and a skeptical Candice decided to start Snowy Peaks Winery in 2004. After months of searching high and low for a building, our future was sealed in Estes Park! We opened our doors in 2005 with no wine of our own but a selection from other Colorado wineries. We bought grapes from growers on the Western Slope that fall and released our first wine in 2006. Since then we have steadily increased the quantity and variety of our offerings.

During the summer season, we generally have 18 Snowy Peaks wines to taste, plus an array of other Colorado wines. Our focus has always been on small batches of well-crafted wines, with a diversity of styles that appeal to all palates. Our tasting room staff tries to keep tastings fun and casual, with the knowledge to educate, if asked.

We believe it's not about us, but you and what you like! Bring the kids along, they will have a great time in the "No Wine-ing Zone," our designated playroom.

TASTING ROOM INFORMATION: Memorial Day to Labor Day, Monday through Saturday from 11 a.m. to 7:00 p.m., Sunday from 12:30 to 6 p.m.; Other times open on weekends, call ahead for hours.

DIRECTIONS: From the intersection of Hwy 34 and Hwy 36 in Estes Park: Head west into downtown Estes Park; turn left (south) onto Moraine Avenue (Hwy 36).

OTHER AMENITIES AT WINERY: Colorado-made food products, handcrafted gifts from local artisans and wine-related merchandise.

WINE AVAILABLE FOR PURCHASE OUTSIDE OF WINERY: Yes

OTHER TASTING ROOM LOCATIONS: No

NOTES: _____

_____

_____

_____

SPERO WINERY

3316 W. 64th Avenue, Denver, CO 80221
720-519-1506
sperowinery.biz
sperowinery@aol.com

OWNER: Clyde and June Spero

YEAR BEGAN OPERATION: 1999

AVERAGE CASES PRODUCED ANNUALLY: 2,100

WINES PRODUCED:
White: Chardonnay, Colombard, Malvasia Bianca, Muscat, Riesling, Viognier
Red: Barbera, Cabernet Franc, Cabernet Sauvignon, Chancellor, Malbec, Merlot, Sangiovese, Syrah, Zinfandel
Other: Blend called Cayuga White, Pomegranate and Dessert wines

MESSAGE FROM OWNER: Spero Winery is a family-owned and operated boutique winery, with wines made in the "Old World" tradition. Clyde Spero, winemaker, has been making wine all of his life; a craft he learned from his father, who emigrated from Potenza, Italy. Our friendly and relaxed tasting room is open Saturdays for free wine tasting. Here you can enjoy the rich and full-bodied wines made more in a European tradition, with our red wines being aged a minimum of two years in oak. We are sure you will find a favorite in the 20 varieties we offer!

There are special case discounts, and don't forget to return the Spero wine bottles for your $1 per bottle credit towards your next purchase. Come enjoy the relaxed, "old country" feel of our tasting room, a great place to bring family and friends!

TASTING ROOM INFORMATION: Saturday from 1 to 5 p.m. or by appointment.

DIRECTIONS: From the intersection of Federal Boulevard and W. 64th Avenue in Denver: Head west on W. 64th Avenue 3 blocks. Winery is on the left (south) side of the street.

OTHER AMENITIES AT WINERY: Private tasting parties for 20–50 people

WINE AVAILABLE FOR PURCHASE OUTSIDE OF WINERY: Yes

OTHER TASTING ROOM LOCATIONS: Winey Bean (see Front Range Region)

NOTES: _____

_____

_____

_____

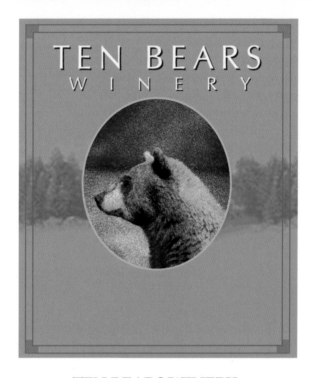

TEN BEARS WINERY

5215 Ten Bears Court, LaPorte, CO 80535
970-566-4043
tenbearswinery.com
tenbearswinery@hotmail.com

OWNER: Bill Conkling

YEAR BEGAN OPERATION: 2006

AVERAGE CASES PRODUCED ANNUALLY: 300

WINES PRODUCED:
White: Chardonnay, Unoaked Chardonnay, Riesling
Red: Cabernet Sauvignon, Merlot
Other: Blends called Cameron Pass White Table Wine, Poudre River
Red Table Wine; Sparkling Riesling

MESSAGE FROM OWNER: Beware of The Ten Bears! Introduce your palate to a truly superior Colorado wine experience. Our winemaker hand selects only the finest grapes. Using French oak aging and our exclusive "Winter Hibernation Process," we produce smooth and flavorful handcrafted vintages that are easy drinking and never overly tannic. Enjoy!

TASTING ROOM INFORMATION: Thursday through Saturday from 11 a.m. to 4p.m.; other days by appointment.

DIRECTIONS: From I-25 at Exit #269 A or B (Hwy 14/Mulberry Street): Head west on Hwy 14/Mulberry Street; turn right (north) onto College Avenue (Hwy 287); turn right (north) and onto Hwy 287 By-Pass (Laramie/Poudre Canyon exit); approximately 4 miles, turn right (northwest) onto CR 56; make an immediate right (northeast) onto 23E; head 1/2 mile to the intersection of 56E and 23E. The winery is a gray building on the right.

OTHER AMENITIES AT WINERY: Home winemaking equipment and other wine items; t-shirts and hats; picnic and patio area; vineyard for touring

WINE AVAILABLE FOR PURCHASE OUTSIDE OF WINERY: Yes

OTHER TASTING ROOM LOCATIONS: No

NOTES: _____

_____

_____

_____

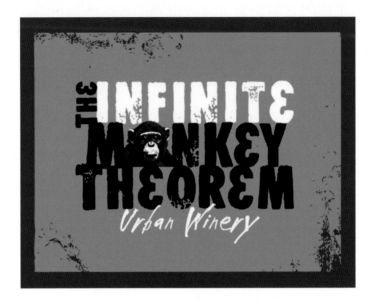

THE INFINITE MONKEY THEOREM

931 W. 5th Avenue, Denver, CO 80204
303-736-8376
theinfinitemonkeytheorem.com
drink@theinfinitemonkeytheorem.com

OWNER: Ben Parsons

YEAR BEGAN OPERATION: 2008

AVERAGE CASES PRODUCED ANNUALLY: 10,000

WINES PRODUCED:
White: Black Muscat, Chardonnay, Gewürztraminer, Riesling,
Rousanne, Viognier
Red: Cabernet Franc, Cabernet Sauvignon, Malbec, Petite Sirah,
Petit Verdot, Syrah
Other: Rosé and Blends called The Blindwatchmaker
and The 100th Monkey

MESSAGE FROM OWNER: Opened in 2008 in Denver, Colorado, The Infinite Monkey Theorem is an urban winery operating out of a converted Quonset hut in a back alley of Denver's Santa Fe Arts District. The winery's purpose is to use the best grapes, from the highest quality vineyards, to process excellent wines in the heart of the city.

TASTING ROOM INFORMATION: By appointment only

DIRECTIONS: From the intersection of I-25 and 6th Avenue: Head east on 6th Avenue; turn right (south) onto Kalamath Street; turn left (east) onto 5th Avenue. Winery is on the left (north) side of the street.

OTHER AMENITIES AT WINERY: Private parties

WINE AVAILABLE FOR PURCHASE OUTSIDE OF WINERY: Yes

OTHER TASTING ROOM LOCATIONS: No

NOTES: _____

_____

_____

_____

Broomfield, Colorado

TURQUOISE MESA WINERY
555 Burbank Street, Unit Q, Broomfield, CO 80020
303-653-3822
turquoisemesawinery.com
tabwine@aol.com

OWNER: Tom & Mary Joan Bueb

YEAR BEGAN OPERATION: 2004

AVERAGE CASES PRODUCED ANNUALLY: 1,000

WINES PRODUCED:
White: Chardonnay, Muscat Blanc, Riesling
Red: Black Muscat, Cabernet Franc, Cabernet Sauvignon, Merlot,
Mourvèdre, Petit Sirah, Syrah
Other: Blends called Sunset White, Colorado Crimson, TMW Reserve,
Vino Turchese, Dessert wines

MESSAGE FROM OWNER: We are a boutique, handcrafted winery. All of our wines are made using only the finest grapes from the Western Slope of Colorado. We offer a wide variety of both red and white wines, including many excellent blends in the Bordeaux and Meritage styles. Come and enjoy our friendly atmosphere and award-winning wines!

TASTING ROOM INFORMATION: Friday and Saturday from 1 to 5 p.m.; Check website for seasonal times/changes. Other times by appointment.

DIRECTIONS: From the intersection of Hwy 36 and Hwy 121/287: Head north on Hwy 121/287; turn left (west) onto W. Midway Boulevard; turn right (north) onto Burbank Street; turn left (west) into the Burbank Business Park halfway down the block.

OTHER AMENITIES AT WINERY: N/A

WINE AVAILABLE FOR PURCHASE OUTSIDE OF WINERY: Yes

OTHER TASTING ROOM LOCATIONS: Seven Arrows Gallery (see Pikes Peak Region)

NOTES: _____

_____

_____

_____

VERSO CELLARS
4640 Pecos Street, Denver, CO 80211
Mailing address: 290 W. 12th Avenue #405, Denver, CO 80204
303-587-9740
versocellars.com
wine@versocellars.com

OWNER: Paul Phillips

YEAR BEGAN OPERATION: 2001

AVERAGE CASES PRODUCED ANNUALLY: 2,000

WINES PRODUCED:
White: None
Red: Cabernet Sauvignon
Other: None

MESSAGE FROM OWNER: Verso Cellars is Colorado's finest 100% Cabernet Sauvignon winery. We grow six varieties of Cabernet grapes, and expertly blend them to craft an extraordinary wine. Our vineyard in East Orchard Mesa makes the most of abundant sunshine, careful attention and precious water to bring you something you may have missed, an excellent Cabernet Sauvignon.

Come visit us at our Tasting Room for a sampling of our delicious Cabernet!

TASTING ROOM INFORMATION: Thursday through Saturday from 1 to 5 p.m.

DIRECTIONS: From I-70 at Exit #273 (Pecos Street): Head south on Pecos; turn left (east) into Colorado Winery Row parking lot (by Quiznos), which is just before 46th Avenue.

OTHER AMENITIES AT WINERY: Facility is available to rent for event needs.

WINE AVAILABLE FOR PURCHASE OUTSIDE OF WINERY: Yes

OTHER TASTING ROOM LOCATIONS: Metropolis Coffee (see Front Range Region)

NOTES: _____

_____

_____

_____

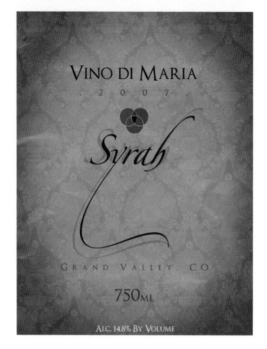

VINO di MARIA
Denver, CO
303-638-3171
vinodimaria.com
info@vinodimaria.com

OWNER: David di Maria

YEAR BEGAN OPERATION: 2007

AVERAGE CASES PRODUCED ANNUALLY: 250

WINES PRODUCED:
White: Chardonnay
Red: Merlot, Syrah
Other: None

MESSAGE FROM OWNER: We are an urban winery in Denver, specializing in highlighting the wonderful fruit from Palisade, Colorado. Our goal is to provide quality local wine at a reasonable price, which is accessible to a wide range of palates. We strive to minimize contact with the wine, so that each vintage is a full expression of time and place.

TASTING ROOM INFORMATION: N/A

DIRECTIONS: N/A

OTHER AMENITIES AT WINERY: N/A

WINE AVAILABLE FOR PURCHASE OUTSIDE OF WINERY: Yes

OTHER TASTING ROOM LOCATIONS: No

NOTES: _____

_____

_____

_____

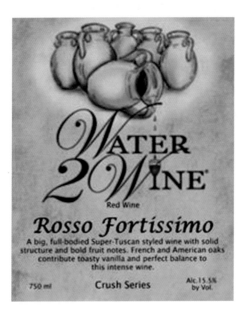

WATER2WINE - CENTENNIAL

8130 S. University Boulevard #110, Centennial, CO 80122

720-489-9463

Water2Wine.com/denver

denver@water2wine.com

OWNER: Derek and Rebecca Handley

YEAR BEGAN OPERATION: 2006

AVERAGE CASES PRODUCED ANNUALLY: 2,500

WINES PRODUCED:
White: Numerous
Red: Numerous
Other: Over 80 varietals and blends to choose from daily

MESSAGE FROM OWNER: We are a locally-owned and operated small business with over 80 wines to choose from, all of which are available for tasting. All of our wines have 20 times fewer sulfites and have no histamines. We source from over 100 vineyards in 14 countries.

For sale by the glass, bottle, or become the vintner and produce your own batch (28 bottles) of wine including custom labels. Great for client gifts, weddings or corporate events.

TASTING ROOM INFORMATION: Tuesday through Friday from 11 a.m. to 7 p.m., Saturday from 11 a.m. to 6 p.m.

DIRECTIONS: From C-470 and University Boulevard: Head north on University Boulevard 2 blocks; winery is on the right (east) side of the street.

OTHER AMENITIES AT WINERY: Available to rent for various events, parties and fund-raisers.

WINE AVAILABLE FOR PURCHASE OUTSIDE OF WINERY: Yes

OTHER TASTING ROOM LOCATIONS: No

NOTES: _____

_____

_____

_____

WATER2WINE - DTC
9608 E. Arapahoe Road, Greenwood Village, CO 80112
303-799-9463
Water2Wine.com/dtc
dtc@water2wine.com

OWNER: Marcus Tipton

YEAR BEGAN OPERATION: 2010

AVERAGE CASES PRODUCED ANNUALLY: Information not Available

WINES PRODUCED:
White: Chardonnay, Chenin Blanc, Pinot Gris, Riesling, Viognier
Red: Amarone, Barolo, Cabernet Sauvignon, Carmenere, Malbec, Merlot, Pinot Noir, Shiraz, Tempranillo, Zinfandel
Other: Over 100 varietals and blends, including Ice wines

MESSAGE FROM OWNER: Enjoy our wines by the glass, bottle, or become the winemaker and create your own wine complete with custom labels! We are a fully operational winery located in the heart of the Denver Tech Center in Greenwood Village. All of our wines are fermented on site. With access to more than 100 wines from 15 countries and everything open for tasting, your taste buds can travel through Colorado and around the world without ever leaving our winery!

Experiences are the things people never forget, so if you are looking for something NEW to do with friends, it is happening at Water2Wine-DTC! We are more creative than a winery and more fun than a wine store, as we offer a fun, laid-back atmosphere where you can learn about wines. We help you create memorable experiences by putting you to work in the winery making your own wine, with friends, and complete with a custom label. Visit our custom winery today and uncork the experience of wine tasting and making a custom label wine...pouring on the fun with Water2Wine-DTC!

TASTING ROOM INFORMATION: Tuesday through Saturday from noon to 8 p.m.

DIRECTIONS: From I-25 and Exit #197 (Arapahoe Road): Head east on Arapahoe Road 2 ½ blocks; turn right (south) onto Clinton Court; turn left (east) into the parking area.

OTHER AMENITIES AT WINERY: Available to rent for various events with A/V equipment available; Wine-related merchandise; create and personalize your own wines; monthly Wine Club exclusive parties.

WINE AVAILABLE FOR PURCHASE OUTSIDE OF WINERY: Yes

OTHER TASTING ROOM LOCATIONS: No

NOTES: _____

_____

_____

_____

ZEPHYR CELLLARS
200 SW 12th Street, Unit 102, Loveland, CO 80537
970-635-0949
Website: N/A
zephyrcellars@yahoo.com

OWNER: Tim Merrick

YEAR BEGAN OPERATION: 2009

AVERAGE CASES PRODUCED ANNUALLY: Information not Available

WINES PRODUCED:
White: Gewürztraminer, Muscat Blanc, Riesling
Red: Cabernet Franc, Zinfandel
Other: Dry Rosé of Cabernet Franc

MESSAGE FROM OWNER: Winemaker, Tim Merrick, has been producing Colorado wines in Loveland, Colorado since 1994. Zephyr Cellars wines are sold through northern Colorado liquor stores in Loveland, Fort Collins, Greeley, Estes Park and Westminster.

TASTING ROOM INFORMATION: Not open to the public

DIRECTIONS: N/A

OTHER AMENITIES AT WINERY: N/A

WINE AVAILABLE FOR PURCHASE OUTSIDE OF WINERY: Yes

OTHER TASTING ROOM LOCATIONS: No

NOTES: _____

_____

_____

_____

FRONT RANGE REGION
What Else To See & Do

The area from Denver to Fort Collins, just east of the Rocky Mountains, is called the Front Range, and has something to offer everyone. Below is just a sampling of the 1,000+ things to see and do in this region. See individual cities and their websites for additional activities and information.

Arts and Museums   see city websites below
From Picasso to Playwrights, there are hundreds of galleries, museums and performing centers along the Front Range. Here are just a few.
- Clyfford Still Museum   clyffordstillmuseum.org
- Denver Art Museum   denverartmuseum.org
- Denver Center for the Performing Arts   denvercenter.org
- Denver Museum of Nature and Science   dmns.org

Beer   mountainbrewbook.com
Tired of wine? While that would be hard to believe, the Front Range offers tours and tastings at the big breweries - Anheuser-Busch, Coors, Odell and New Belgium, and at numerous micro-breweries.

Boulder   bouldercoloradousa.com

Butterfly Pavilion   butterflies.org
A tarantula walks on your hand? A butterfly lands on your head? Just some things to experience at this invertebrate and conservation center.

Colorado Renaissance Festival   coloradorenaissance.com
Step back in time to 16th Century England at this summer festival featuring costumed merrymakers and artisans.

Colorado State Capitol   colorado.gov/capitoltour
Find out where Colorado's laws are made and view the House and Senate galleries. You can tour the capitol building and learn about its history and construction.

Denver   denver.org

Denver Botanic Gardens   denverbotanicgardens.org

Get out your cameras or sketch pads and take a walk through the beautiful and innovative gardens that highlight plants from all over the world.

Denver Zoo   denverzoo.org

Lions and tigers and bears, oh my! Enjoy this top attraction located on 80 acres in City Park, featuring over 4,000 animals.

Downtown Aquarium   aquariumrestaurants.com

Swim little fishy, swim! That's what you will see at this entertainment and dining complex featuring 500+ species of aquatic life and other animals.

Elitch Gardens Theme Park   elitchgardens.com

Dive, corkscrew, twist and turn at this 70-acre amusement park featuring thrill, family, kid and water rides.

Evergreen   evergreenchamber.org
Estes Park   estesparkcvb.com
Fort Collins   visit.ftcollins.com

Gambling   centralcitycolorado.com / cityofblackhawk.org

Is Lady Luck on your side? Find out at these casinos.

History   historycolorado.org

Learn about when the West was wild and mining was predominant.
- Buffalo Bill Museum and Grave   buffalobill.org
- Byers-Evans House   historycolorado.org/museums
- History Colorado Center   historycolorado.org/museums
- Molly Brown House   mollybrown.org

Red Rocks Amphitheatre & Visitors Center   redrocksonline.com

What bands played at Red Rocks in 1975? 1985? 2005? Find out at the Performer's Hall of Fame. In addition to their summer concert series, the Park offers hiking and biking trails and spectacular vistas.

Rocky Mountain National Park   nps.gov/romo

From elk's bugling to hiking trails to the magnificent views on Trail Ridge Road, RMNP is truly nature's wonderland!

Sports

If you are thinking sports, the Front Range has them all:

- Colorado Avalanche (hockey)   avalanche.nhl.com
- Colorado Mammoth (lacrosse)   coloradomammoth.com
- Colorado Rapids (soccer)   coloradorapids.com
- Colorado Rockies (baseball)   colorado.rockies.mlb.com
- Denver Broncos (football)   denverbroncos.com
- Denver Nuggets (basketball)   nba.com/nuggets
- Denver Outlaws (lacrosse)   denveroutlaws.com

U.S. Mint   usmint.gov/mint_tours

Learn how to make money! Discover how your coins are made and what the little "D" stands for during your tour.

FRONT RANGE REGION
Additional Tasting Locations

Aspen Peak Cellars at Clifton House Inn (Aspen Peak Cellars)
12414 Hwy 285, Conifer, CO 80433
303-816-5505
aspenpeakcellars.com
Owner: Marcel and Julie Flukiger
Hours: Monday, Wednesday, Thursday, Saturday, Sunday
from 10 a.m. to 5 p.m., Friday from 10 a.m. to 8 p.m.

Coffee at the Point (Cottonwood Cellars/The Olathe Winery)
710 E. 26th Avenue, Denver, CO 80205
303-955-2237
coffeeatthepoint.com
Owner: Ryan Gobbins
Hours: Daily from 10 a.m. to 9 p.m.

Metropolis Coffee (Verso Cellars)
300 W. 11th Street, Denver, CO 80204
303-524-1744
metropolisdenver.com
Owner: Brock Wortman
Hours: Monday through Saturday from 7 a.m. to 8 p.m.,
Sunday from 7 a.m. to 6 p.m.

Palma Cigars (Woody Creek Cellars)
2207 Larimer Street, Denver CO 80205
303-297-3244
palmacigars.com
Owner: Clay Carlton
Hours: Tuesday through Saturday from 11 a.m. to 10 p.m.

Shangri-La (Sutcliffe Vineyards)

1575 Boulder Street, Denver, CO 80211
720-855-7585
shangriladenver.com
Owner: Massimo Ruffinazzi
Hours: Monday through Friday from 6 a.m. to 8 p.m.,
Saturday from 7 a.m. to 6 p.m., Sunday from 8 a.m. to 3 p.m.

Tewksbury and Company (Plum Creek Cellars, various other wineries)

1512 Larimer Street, Denver, CO 80202
303-825-1880
tewksburycompany.com
Owner: Dave Tewksbury
Hours: Daily from 1:30 to 5 p.m.

The Winey Bean (Spero Winery)

3937 Tennyson, Denver, CO 80212
720-328-6362
thewineybean.com
Owner: Annette Swenson
Hours: Tuesday through Saturday from 8 a.m. to 6 p.m.,
Sunday from 8 a.m. to 2 p.m.

Pikes Peak Region

Wine Fact

Labels were first put on
wine bottles in the early 1700s,
but it wasn't until the 1860s
that suitable glues were developed
to hold them on the bottles.

http://www.beekmanwine.com/factsquotes.htm

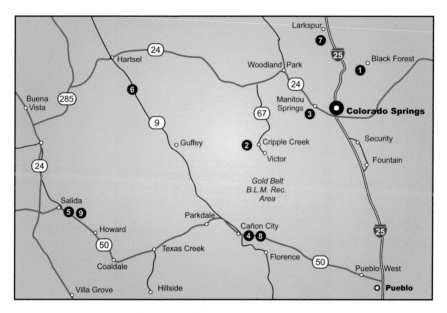

Pikes Peak Region Wineries

1. Black Forest Meadery
2. Byerscellars Wines
3. D'Vine Wine - Manitou Springs
4. LeFuselier Winery @ Spring Creek Vineyards
5. Mountain Spirit Winery
6. Rockyspring Winery
7. Spruce Mountain Meadery
8. The Winery at Holy Cross Abbey
9. Vino Salida Wine Cellars

BLACK FOREST MEADERY

6420 Burrows Road, Unit A, Colorado Springs, CO 80908
719-495-7340
blackforestmeadery.com
mail@blackforestmeadery.com

OWNER: Brad and Shawna Shapiro

YEAR BEGAN OPERATION: 2007

AVERAGE CASES PRODUCED ANNUALLY: Information not Available

WINES PRODUCED:
White: None
Red: None
Other: Meads called: Melody in the Meadows (sweet, honey wine),
Mead in the Woods (dry, golden mead) and Forest Mead (light mead)

MESSAGE FROM OWNER: The company was created in 2007 and is owned/operated by the Shapiro family. The sons (aka The Two Brothers) help in the planting of the vines, which were first started in pots. We thought, "Let's see what grows." We were surprised and impressed by the vines that can grow at 7,500' in Colorado. Typically, vines will grow 1.5' in the first growing year. Our vines grow around 5' in length, due to the soil and intense sunlight.

The vineyard is an experiment, and the experiment is a lesson in pride, delight, struggle and success. We have had good years and bad, but continue to research, test and gather results. Currently we are growing over 600 vines. Come visit our tasting room and delight in what we can produce!

TASTING ROOM INFORMATION: Memorial Day weekend to October, Thursday through Sunday from noon to 4 p.m.; other times by appointment only.

DIRECTIONS: From the intersection of I-25 at Exit #153, north of Colorado Springs: Exit at #153 onto Hwy 83 (Interquest Parkway); turn right (south) onto N. Powers Boulevard (Hwy 21); turn left (east) onto Old Ranch Road; turn left (north) onto Milam Road; turn right (east) onto Burgess Road; turn left (north) onto Burrows Road..

OTHER AMENITIES AT WINERY: T-shirts and trivets

WINE AVAILABLE FOR PURCHASE OUTSIDE OF WINERY: Yes

OTHER TASTING ROOM LOCATIONS: Vintage Vines (see Pikes Peak Region)

NOTES: _____

_____

_____

_____

BYERSCELLARS WINES
109 W. Galena Avenue, Cripple Creek, CO 80813
303-570-5536
cripplecreekcellars.com
byerscellars@aol.com

OWNER: Nancy Byers

YEAR BEGAN OPERATION: 2010

AVERAGE CASES PRODUCED ANNUALLY: Information not Available

WINES PRODUCED:
White: Chardonnay
Red: Merlot
Other: Peach Chardonnay, Chocolate Cherry Merlot

MESSAGE FROM OWNER: High up in the Rocky Mountains there's a winery…Byerscellars Wines, LLC, which is a one-woman winery. It is located in the old western mining and gambling town of Cripple Creek, just west of Pikes Peak, at an elevation of 9,495'. We are dedicated to creating specialty wines in small batch production.

Byerscellars Wines makes some of the most unique and flavorful wines in Colorado. Our Peach Chardonnay is made with Palisade peaches and is a 100% Colorado product. What can we say about our Chocolate Cherry Merlot? It is a delicious combination of chocolate extract flavors and cherry, in the form of Montmorency Cherry juice, which has the perfect sweet/tart taste. One thing is for certain, the fantastic flavors will explode in your mouth. Make an appointment today to taste our delicious wines!

TASTING ROOM INFORMATION: By appointment only

DIRECTIONS: Provided at time of tasting appointment confirmation.

OTHER AMENITIES AT WINERY: N/A

WINE AVAILABLE FOR PURCHASE OUTSIDE OF WINERY: No

OTHER TASTING ROOM LOCATIONS: No

NOTES: _____

_____

_____

_____

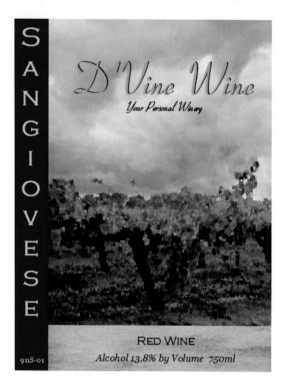

D'VINE WINE - MANITOU SPRINGS

934 Manitou Avenue #108, Manitou Springs, CO 80829
719-685-1030
winerymsprings.com
winery@winerymsprings.com

OWNER: Dean and Tracy Fagner

YEAR BEGAN OPERATION: 2008

AVERAGE CASES PRODUCED ANNUALLY: 3,000

WINES PRODUCED:
White: Chardonnay, Pinot Grigio, Sauvignon Blanc
Red: Merlot, Pinot Noir, Sangiovese, Syrah
Other: Numerous red blends, Fruit wines, Port wines, Ice wine

MESSAGE FROM OWNER: D'Vine Wine-Manitou Springs is a boutique winery located in the historic spa building, in the heart of Manitou Springs. We import the highest quality grapes and then handcraft, blend and ferment all of our wines right in front of you! Drop in and enjoy a wine tasting, a glass of wine, or pick up a bottle.

Want to create a custom blend that is all your own? Our staff can guide you through making your very own wine! In addition to having a custom blend, you can enjoy a bottling party with friends, and each bottle will have your own personalized label.

TASTING ROOM INFORMATION: Monday through Saturday from noon to 8 p.m., Sunday from noon to 7 p.m.

DIRECTIONS: From the intersection of I-25 and Exit #141(Cimarron Street) in Colorado Springs: Head west towards Manitou Springs on Cimarron Street (Hwy 24); take the first exit on the right for Manitou Springs, which is just past 31st Street; winery is on the west end of historic downtown next to the Penny Arcade.

OTHER AMENITIES AT WINERY: Wine-related merchandise and light appetizers. We are available for private parties, events and weddings. Art work is available for purchase. We allow our customers to make their own wine and bottle it when it is ready.

WINE AVAILABLE FOR PURCHASE OUTSIDE OF WINERY: Yes

OTHER TASTING ROOM LOCATIONS: Four Leaves Winery (see Four Corners Region)

NOTES: _____

_____

_____

_____

On label:
Le Fuselier

750 ML.

CONTAINS SULFITES

12% ALC./VOL.

GOVERNMENT WARNING: (1) ACCORDING TO THE SURGEON GENERAL, WOMEN SHOULD NOT DRINK ALCOHOLIC BEVERAGES DURING PREGNANCY BECAUSE OF THE RISK OF BIRTH DEFECTS. (2) CONSUMPTION OF ALCOHOLIC BEVERAGES IMPAIRS YOUR ABILITY TO DRIVE A CAR OR OPERATE MACHINERY, AND MAY CAUSE HEALTH PROBLEMS.

2010 COLORADO
CAYUGA WHITE
From Spring Creek Vineyards, 1702 Willow St.
Canon City, CO www.LeFuselier.com

LE FUSELIER WINERY @
SPRING CREEK VINEYARDS
1702 Willow Street, Cañon City, CO 81212
719-315-2075
LeFuselier.com
or ColoradoGrapes.com
David@ColoradoGrapes.com

OWNER: David Fuselier

YEAR BEGAN OPERATION: 2009

AVERAGE CASES PRODUCED ANNUALLY: 500

WINES PRODUCED:
White: Pinot Grigio, Pinot Gris, Riesling
Red: Cabernet Sauvignon, Reserve Merlot
Other: Blends called Old World Blend, Cayuga White; Frontenac Nouveau, as well as many others

MESSAGE FROM OWNER: The Le Fuselier Winery at Spring Creek Vineyards is a small, family-operated village winery producing more than 30 different wines annually. David and Karin Fuselier make most of their wine from grapes they grow themselves or from 20 contract growers around town. Cañon City was settled by Italian immigrants, who brought grapes to grow in the city's remarkable, fruit-friendly climate, created by its position in a cul de sac cut into the Front Range of the Rockies. The Fuselier's hillside vineyard was hand-terraced to grow grapes more than 100 years ago and currently produces 13 different varieties.

TASTING ROOM INFORMATION: May, September through December, Saturday from noon to 5 p.m.

DIRECTIONS: From the intersection of Hwy 50 and Mackenzie Avenue on the east side of Cañon City: Head south on Mackenzie Avenue; turn right (northwest) onto Hwy 115. The winery is at the intersection of Hwy 115 and Willow Street.

OTHER AMENITIES AT WINERY: N/A

WINE AVAILABLE FOR PURCHASE OUTSIDE OF WINERY: No

OTHER TASTING ROOM LOCATIONS: Studio West Aveda (see Pikes Peak Region)

NOTES: _____

_____

_____

_____

MOUNTAIN SPIRIT WINERY

15750 County Road 220, Salida, CO 81201
Mailing address: 16150 County Road 220, Salida, CO 81201
719-539-1175
mountainspiritwinery.com
barkett@mountainspiritwinery.com

OWNER: Terry and Michael Barkett

YEAR BEGAN OPERATION: 1995

AVERAGE CASES PRODUCED ANNUALLY: 2,500

WINES PRODUCED:
White: None
Red: None
Other: Unique blends with grapes and fruits: Riesling/Chardonnay,
Sophie's White, Blackberry/Cabernet Franc, Merlot/Raspberry,
Sophie's Red, Angel Blush, Dessert wines and Ice wine

MESSAGE FROM OWNER: Mountain Spirit Winery is a family-owned and operated boutique winery nestled in the high country of Colorado's Upper Arkansas Valley. Five acres of farmland, replete with apple orchards and an old homestead house, surrounded by 14,000' mountain vistas, establish the ambience for making Mountain Spirit premium wines. We have won over 50 national and international awards for our wines.

Co-winemakers Terry and Michael Barkett, bring educational backgrounds of clinical medicine, laboratory technology and computer science to the winemaker's art. The winemakers continue to push the limits of exploring new blends of wines, while maintaining the traditional, historic, high standards inherent to the gentle art of winemaking, giving rise to their motto: "Quality Wines, with a Difference."

TASTING ROOM INFORMATION: Summer, daily, from 10 a.m. to 5 p.m.; Winter, Monday through Saturday from 10 a.m. to 5 p.m.

DIRECTIONS: From the intersection of Hwy 285 and Hwy 50 north of Poncha Springs: Head west on Hwy 50; just before the town of Maysville, turn left (south) at the second County Road 220 turnoff; make an immediate left (east) onto County Road 220. The winery is just down the road.

OTHER AMENITIES AT WINERY: Picnic beneath 14,000' mountain peaks!

WINE AVAILABLE FOR PURCHASE OUTSIDE OF WINERY: No

OTHER TASTING ROOM LOCATIONS: Mountain Spirit Winery & Gallery (see Pikes Peak Region)

NOTES: _____

_____

_____

_____

ROCKYSPRING WINERY
1339 Wolfe Road, Hartsel, CO 80449
Winery: 719-837-2044, Denver area: 303-343-7454
rockyspringwinery.com
sales@rockyspringwinery.com

OWNER: Carlson Family

YEAR BEGAN OPERATION: 2009

AVERAGE CASES PRODUCED ANNUALLY: Information not Available

WINES PRODUCED:
White: Peach Apricot Chardonnay, Pinot Grigio, Green Apple Riesling, Riesling
Red: Cabernet Franc, Blackberry Cabernet, Pinot Noir, Sangiovese, Colorado Mountain Shiraz, Rockyspring Shiraz, Sweet Petite Sirah, Very Berry Shiraz, Red Zinfandel
Other: Blends called Muller Thurgau, Tropical Fruit Fuzion; White Zinfandel/Ice wine, Dessert wines and Port wines

MESSAGE FROM OWNER: Rockyspring Winery is a family-owned and operated winery/vineyard located in Park County, Colorado (South Park). We are dedicated to producing the highest quality, hand-crafted, artisan wines possible. All our wines are produced in limited quantities each year, based upon the quantity of grapes we are able to grow and the grapes we are able to obtain from other vineyards in Colorado. Each year increasing the number of vines in our vineyards, we look forward to all our wines being labeled "100% Colorado."

With the experience of four generations of winemakers, we feel you will find our wines to be a wonderful change from the everyday wines you may have experienced. Our production levels are intentionally small, but our quality is superb. We ask only that you try our wine, we truly believe you will like one or all of our superb wines.

TASTING ROOM INFORMATION: Mid-March through early November, Wednesday through Saturday from 10 a.m. to 7 p.m., Sunday from 10 a.m. to 6 p.m.; early November through mid-March, Thursday through Saturday from 10 a.m. to 5 p.m., Sunday from 10 a.m. to 5 p.m.; other times by appointment.

DIRECTIONS: From the intersection of Hwy 24 and Hwy 9 in Hartsel: Head south on Hwy 9, approximately 12 miles; turn right (west) onto Wolfe Road (MM35); continue 1.5 miles to winery. Wolfe Road is not an all-weather road, call ahead for conditions.

OTHER AMENITIES AT WINERY: A gift shop displaying local artisans' products for purchase. We are planning outdoor events in the future: concerts, grape picking and events for school groups.

WINE AVAILABLE FOR PURCHASE OUTSIDE OF WINERY: Yes

OTHER TASTING ROOM LOCATIONS: No

NOTES: _____

_____

_____

_____

SPRUCE MOUNTAIN MEADERY

1218 Yarnell Drive, Larkspur, CO 80118

855-GET-MEAD (438-6323)

sprucemountainmeadery.com

info@sprucemountainmeadery.com

OWNER: Gretchen and Harrison Bliss

YEAR BEGAN OPERATION: 2003

AVERAGE CASES PRODUCED ANNUALLY: 600

WINES PRODUCED:

White: None

Red: None

Other: Meads - Traditional, Fruit (Blackberry) and Spiced (Cinnamon and Nutmeg)

MESSAGE FROM OWNER: Spruce Mountain Meadery is located at the foot of Spruce Mountain just south of Larkspur, Colorado. The smell of the pines, the rustle of the aspens, the serenity of the deep snow and visits from the local wildlife create the perfect atmosphere for developing our exceptional meads. We are a 'micro-winery' handcrafting our meads in small batches. We got our taste for mead-making while travelling in Europe, as we were fascinated by the family wineries and loved the taste of the local mead. We combined the two experiences, and Spruce Mountain Meadery was born!

Each of our meads is made from the finest ingredients available. We pasteurize our meads to retain the essence of our ingredients, and we do not add sulfites, out of respect for our friends with sulfite allergies. We are reviving the ancient art of making mead with all of its mystery and nobility. Please come and visit us soon to sample the ancient beverage of kings!

TASTING ROOM INFORMATION: By appointment only

DIRECTIONS: From I-25 and Exit #167 just south of Larkspur: Head west on Hwy 74 (Greenland Road, which changes name to Noe Road); turn left (south) on Hwy 105 (Perry Park Road); turn left onto Yarnell Drive

OTHER AMENITIES AT WINERY: N/A

WINE AVAILABLE FOR PURCHASE OUTSIDE OF WINERY: Yes

OTHER TASTING ROOM LOCATIONS: No

NOTES: _____

_____

_____

_____

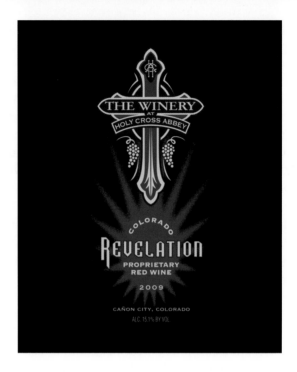

THE WINERY AT HOLY CROSS ABBEY
3011 E. Hwy 50, Cañon City, CO 81212
719-276-5191 or 877-422-9463 (HCA-WINE)
abbeywinery.com
sally@abbeywinery.com

OWNER: Larry and Diane Oddo and Sally Davidson

YEAR BEGAN OPERATION: 2001

AVERAGE CASES PRODUCED ANNUALLY: 14,000

WINES PRODUCED:
White: Chardonnay, Riesling, Sauvignon Blanc Reserve
Red: Cabernet Franc, Cabernet Sauvignon, Cabernet Sauvignon
Reserve, Merlot, Merlot Reserve, Syrah
Other: Blends called Revelation, Sangre de Cristo Nouveau, Vineyard
Sunset, Wild Cañon Harvest, Apple Blossom, Merlot Divinity

MESSAGE FROM OWNER: Eleven years ago some simple Benedictine Fathers had a dream. Today that dream is a reality! The Winery at Holy Cross Abbey was built by Sally Davidson and Matt Cookson in 2001, and it is now the largest and oldest winery in Cañon City, Colorado.

We carry 15 different wines, most of which are available year-round. All our wines are complimentary to sample in the tasting room, except the reserve wines, which are $1 each to taste.

Our wine selection caters to every taste, with an array from dry white, to dry red, to our sweeter series of wines. All of our wines have won numerous international awards.

TASTING ROOM INFORMATION: April through December, Monday through Saturday from 10 a.m. to 6 p.m., Sunday from noon to 5 p.m.; January through March, Monday through Saturday from 10 a.m. to 5 p.m., Sunday from noon to 5 p.m.

DIRECTIONS: From the intersection of Hwy 50 and Mackenzie Avenue in eastern Cañon City: Head west on Hwy 50. The Winery is located just west of Dozier Avenue.

OTHER AMENITIES AT WINERY: Park facilities

WINE AVAILABLE FOR PURCHASE OUTSIDE OF WINERY: Yes

OTHER TASTING ROOM LOCATIONS: No

NOTES: _____

_____

_____

_____

VINO SALIDA WINE CELLARS

8100 W. Hwy 50, Unit B, Salida, CO 81201
Mailing address: PO Box 43, Salida, CO 81201
719-539-6299
vinosalida.com
steve@vinosalida.com

OWNER: Steve Flynn

YEAR BEGAN OPERATION: 2009

AVERAGE CASES PRODUCED ANNUALLY: 1,500

WINES PRODUCED:
White: Riesling, Viognier
Red: Merlot, Petite Sirah, Syrah
Other: Blends called Vino Bianco di Salida, Vino Rosso di Salida,
Vino Rosato di Salida, Vino Novello di Salida; Bee Vino, a honey mead.

MESSAGE FROM OWNER: Opened in 2009 in Salida, Colorado, Vino Salida Wine Cellars is a small, artisan winery in the heart of the Colorado Rocky Mountains. Steve Flynn, winemaker/owner, caught the "wine bug" in 2002 when he experienced his first grape crush while working for Mountain Spirit Winery. He works closely with grape growers in Palisade and Paonia, a local honey producer and a small cooperage in Kentucky to produce unique varietals and tasty blends.

At harvest, Steve's goal is to express the grower's art by encouraging a slow and natural fermentation, slowly allowing the wines to showcase their own personality in the glass. The result is a true reflection of Colorado terroir that pairs well with local foods. The wines are inviting to the palate, full of character, flavor and body that linger from start to finish, leaving you with a desire to taste more! When you enter the Vino Salida Tasting Parlour, you are welcomed by friendly staff and will be offered wine tasting and a casual winery tour.

TASTING ROOM INFORMATION: Monday through Saturday from 10 a.m. to 6 p.m., Sunday from noon to 5 p.m.

DIRECTIONS: From the intersection of Hwy 50 and Holman Avenue in Salida: Head west on Hwy 50. The Winery is just past Wal-Mart on the right (north) side in a 4-plex metal building.

OTHER AMENITIES AT WINERY: Custom wine tasting events for up to 20 people in the Barrel Room.

WINE AVAILABLE FOR PURCHASE OUTSIDE OF WINERY: Yes

OTHER TASTING ROOM LOCATIONS: Wanderlust Road (see Pikes Peak Region)

NOTES: _____

_____

_____

_____

PIKES PEAK REGION
What Else To See & Do

Cave of the Winds   caveofthewinds.com
Head underground into a mile of caverns that were discovered in 1881.
Three educational tours of varying lengths and difficulty help you explore
these cave formations by flashlight or hand-held lanterns.

Cheyenne Mountain Zoo   cmzoo.org
Give an 18" long giraffe tongue a cookie? You can at this zoo, which
combines breathtaking scenery with more than 700 animals. Your
admission ticket includes the spectacular drive to the Will Rogers Shrine
built in the 1930s.

Colorado Springs Sky Sox   minorleaguebaseball.com
"Take me out to the ball game." The Colorado Springs Sky Sox are the
AAA affiliate of the Colorado Rockies. Day or night games are available.

Florissant Fossil Beds National Monument   nps.gov/flfo
Stretch your legs and take a short, self-guided walk around this exciting
fossil deposit. The park and Visitor Center display fossil deposits, massive
petrified redwood trees and fossils of insects and leaves.

Gambling   visitcripplecreek.com
Try your luck and seek your fortune at one of the many casinos in Cripple
Creek. You can also travel back in time to the Gold Rush days in this
historic town, which offers breathtaking views, mine tours and shopping.

Garden of the Gods Visitor & Nature Center   gardenofgods.com
"How Did Those Red Rocks Get There?" Watch the movie at the Visitor
Center and find out, then explore the magnificent 300' towering sandstone
rock formations. Pikes Peak is the backdrop to this national landmark.

Outdoor Activities
- **Hiking, Biking and '14ers**   trails.com & numerous websites
  There are hundreds of trails in the Pikes Peak region. Interested
  in climbing a 14,000' mountain? Chaffee County is home to 15!

- **Rafting**   canoncitycolorado.com

Sense the adrenaline rush as you paddle down the Arkansas River! This website provides a list of companies offering rafting trips and adventures.

Pikes Peak   pikespeak.us.com

Test your brakes, grip the wheel and then drive the 19-mile Pikes Peak Highway to the 14,115' summit. On a clear day, the 360-degree panorama offers views of Colorado Springs, the eastern plains and the Continental Divide. It was "discovered" by Lt. Zebulon Pike in 1806, and Katharine Lee Bates was inspired to write "America the Beautiful" from its summit.

Pikes Peak Cog Railway   cograilway.com

If you would rather leave the driving to someone else, the cog railroad is your answer! Since 1891, the Railway has transported millions of people along the 9-mile track to the summit of Pikes Peak. Reservations a must!

ProRodeo Hall of Fame   prorodeohalloffame.com

Put on your cowboy/girl boots and visit the only heritage center in the world devoted to professional rodeo. After viewing a history film, visitors can explore the museum that pays tribute to the American cowboy.

Royal Gorge Bridge   royalgorgebridge.com

Are you acrophobic? Then the view from the 956' suspension bridge might be difficult! You can walk across the bridge, as well as ride the aerial tram, the incline railway and enjoy the 21 amusement rides.

Royal Gorge Train   royalgorgeroute.com

"All aboard"…take a ride on the rails behind a 1950s streamliner taking in the scenery of the Royal Gorge and Arkansas River. The train offers several unique options: a lunch or dinner with wine experience, a mystery train and, in December, ride the Polar Express Train.

United States Air Force Academy   usafa.af.mil/information/visitors

Experience the core values of Integrity First, Service Before Self and Excellence In All We Do at the USAF Academy. Visitors may access several areas including the spectacular Cadet Chapel, Falcon Stadium and the Visitor Center.

For further information, please visit these websites:

canoncity.com

canoncitycolorado.com

manitousprings.org

nowthisiscolorado.com

salidachamber.org

salidachamber.org

visitcripplecreek.com

visitcos.com

woodlandparkchamber.com

PIKES PEAK REGION

Additional Tasting Locations

Mountain Spirit Winery and Gallery (Mountain Spirit Winery)

8046 W. Hwy 285, Salida, CO 81201
719-539-7848
mountainspiritwinery.com/gallery
Owner: Mike and Terry Barkett
Hours: Monday through Saturday from 10 a.m. to 5 p.m.

Wanderlust Road (Vino Salida Wine Cellars)

145 W. 1st Street, Salida, CO 81201
719-539-0420
wanderlustroad.com
Owner: Terri and Greg Vroom
Hours: Daily, from noon to 5 p.m.

Wines of Colorado (Minturn Cellars, 75+ other Colorado wineries)

8045 W. Hwy 24, Cascade, CO 80809
719-684-0900
winesofcolorado.com
Owner: Marvin Parliament and Bruce McLaughlin
Hours: Daily, from 10 a.m. to 8:30 p.m.

TASTING ROOMS OF WOODLAND PARK:

Cowbells and the Deersnake Gallery (Cottonwood Cellars/The Olathe Winery)

214 W. Midland Avenue, Woodland Park, CO 80863
719-687-4334
cowbellsgifts.com
Owner: Deb Nichols
Hours: Tuesday through Saturday, all day

Mountain Rains Gallery and Gifts (Dithyramb Vineyards)
220 W. Midland Avenue, Woodland Park, CO 80863
719-641-1557
mountainrains.com
Owner: Laurie Spencer
Hours: generally Monday through Saturday from 11 a.m. to 5: 30 p.m.

Seven Arrows Gallery (Turquoise Mesa Winery)
118 W. Midland Avenue, Woodland Park, CO 80863
719-761-1676
7arrowsgallery.com
Owner: Ralph Holloway
Hours: Monday through Saturday from 10 a.m. to 6 p.m.,
Sunday by appointment only

Studio West Aveda (Le Fuselier @ Spring Creek Vineyards)
216 W. Midland Avenue, Woodland Park, CO 80863
719-687-2599
studiowestaveda.com
Owner: Darlene Holloway
Hours: Monday through Saturday from 9 a.m. to 6 p.m.

Treasures for All Seasons (Aspen Peak Cellars)
102 W. Midland Avenue, Woodland Park, CO 80863
719-686-1409
treasuresforallseasons.biz
Owner: Jamie and Ben Caperton
Hours: Monday through Saturday from 10 a.m. to 5 :30 p.m.,
Sunday from noon to 5 p.m.

Vintage Vines (Black Forest Meadery)
108 W. Midland Avenue, Woodland Park, CO 80863
719-687-4046
website: n/a
Owner: Jan Cummer
Hours: Monday through Saturday from 10 a.m. to 5 p.m.,
Sunday 11 a.m. to 4 p.m.

Mountains Region

Wine Fact

When Tutankhamen's tomb
was opened in 1922, the wine jars
buried with him were labeled
with the year, the name of the
winemaker, and comments such
as "very good wine." The labels
were so specific that they could
actually meet modern wine label
laws of several countries.

http://facts.randomhistory.com/
2009/08/21_wine.html

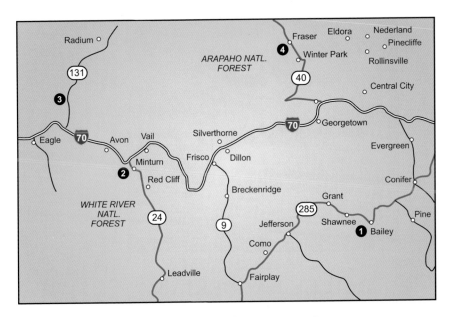

Mountains Region Wineries

1. Aspen Peak Cellars
2. Minturn Cellars
3. Vines at Vail Winery
4. Winter Park Winery

BAILEY BARBERIAN

RED TABLE WINE   ALC 13% BY VOL

PRODUCED AND BOTTLED BY:
ASPEN PEAK CELLARS, INC.
CONIFER, COLORADO
WWW.ASPENPEAKCELLARS.COM

CONTAINS SULFITES
750 ML

GOVERNMENT WARNING: (1) ACCORDING TO THE SURGEON GENERAL, WOMEN SHOULD NOT DRINK ALCOHOLIC BEVERAGES DURING PREGNANCY BECAUSE OF THE RISK OF BIRTH DEFECTS. (2) CONSUMPTION OF ALCOHOLIC BEVERAGES IMPAIRS YOUR ABILITY TO DRIVE A CAR AND OPERATE MACHINERY, AND MAY CAUSE HEALTH PROBLEMS.

ASPEN PEAK CELLARS
60750 US Hwy 285, Bailey, CO 80421
303-816-5505
aspenpeakcellars.com
info@aspenpeakcellars.com

OWNER: Marcel and Julie Flukiger

YEAR BEGAN OPERATION: 2009

AVERAGE CASES PRODUCED ANNUALLY: 1,500

WINES PRODUCED:
White: Chardonnay, Pinot Grigio, Riesling
Red: Barbera, Cabernet Sauvignon, Pinot Noir, Zinfandel
Other: Blend called Conifer Red, Strawberry Rosé, Pomegranate Rouge, Blanc de Blancs (Sparkling wine)

MESSAGE FROM OWNER: Marcel and Julie Flukiger developed a passion for winemaking several years ago, when Marcel bought Julie a winemaking kit for Christmas. The hobby got out of control, and in 2009 they started commercial production at the historic Clifton House Inn in Conifer. The inn includes a tasting room, lunch Bistro and B&B, providing their clientele a wonderful culinary experience, "Celebrating the Art of Food and Wine" as they like to call it. With demand on the rise and production space getting tighter, they moved the winery to downtown Bailey.

Aspen Peak Cellars currently produces a full line of award-winning wines from dry to sweet, light to bold, and even a method champagnoise sparkling wine, pleasing a broad range of wineaux palates, at affordable prices. Whether you stop in at our tasting locations, pick a bottle up at your favorite liquor store or order wine from our Facebook page, we would like to thank you for supporting our local family-owned business and hope you enjoy our passion for wine that you will find in each of our bottles.

TASTING ROOM INFORMATION: Wednesday through Sunday from 11 a.m. to 5 p.m.

DIRECTIONS: From the intersection of Hwy 285 and C-470: South on Hwy 285 to downtown Bailey; turn left (east) onto CR 68; make an immediate right (south) into Rustic Square; turn right (west) by the river and follow driveway to the winery.

OTHER AMENITIES AT WINERY: Gift shop, Winery tours and the Winery is available to rent for private party events.

WINE AVAILABLE FOR PURCHASE OUTSIDE OF WINERY: Yes

OTHER TASTING ROOM LOCATIONS: Clifton House Bed & Breakfast (see Front Range Region), Treasures for all Seasons (see Pikes Peak Region)

NOTES: _____

_____

_____

_____

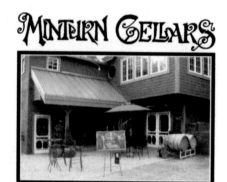

MINTURN CELLARS
107 Williams Street, Minturn, CO 81645
970-827-4746
Website: N/A
Email: N/A

OWNER: Marietta "Taffy" and Bruce McLaughlin

YEAR BEGAN OPERATION: 1990

AVERAGE CASES PRODUCED ANNUALLY: Varies by year

WINES PRODUCED:
White: Viognier
Red: Cabernet Sauvignon, Merlot, Syrah
Other: None

MESSAGE FROM OWNER: Minturn Cellars is located at 7,861'
elevation…believed to be the highest elevation winery in the world.

TASTING ROOM INFORMATION: June through October, daily, from
noon to 4 p.m.

DIRECTIONS: From the intersection of I-70 and Exit #171 (Hwy 24):
Head south on Hwy 24; just as you enter into downtown Minturn, turn
right (south) onto Williams Street.

OTHER AMENITIES AT WINERY: Available to rent for private parties
for up to 25 people, featuring "Tapas and Sangria" parties.

WINE AVAILABLE FOR PURCHASE OUTSIDE OF WINERY: Yes

OTHER TASTING ROOM LOCATIONS: The Wines of Colorado
(see Pikes Peak Region)

NOTES: _____

_____

_____

_____

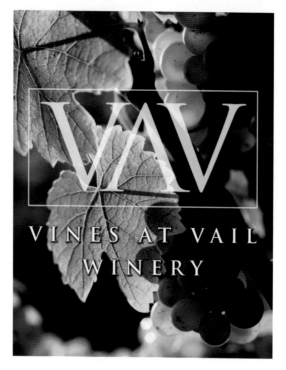

VINES AT VAIL WINERY
4 Eagle Ranch, 4098 Hwy 131, Wolcott, CO 81655
Mailing address: PO Box 18296, Avon, CO 81620
Phone Number: N/A
Website: coming soon
churchre@vail.net

OWNER: Patrick Chirichillo

YEAR BEGAN OPERATION: Spring/Summer 2012

AVERAGE CASES PRODUCED ANNUALLY: 2,000

WINES PRODUCED:
White: None
Red: None
Other: Blends called Chateauneuff du Pape, Cotes du Rhône, Oracle,
Pinnacle, Quartet, Petite Sirah, Super Tuscan

MESSAGE FROM OWNER: We started out based as a "Winemaking Club", where members join us in making their own wine using California grapes. The Winery attracts aspiring winemakers, who assist in all facets of the vinification process. Members purchase their own shares of a barrel and plan on coming to the Winery three times a year for crushing, pressing, bottling, and most importantly, sharing a family tradition with their friends and fellow winemakers.

After 20 years of hand-crafting our award-winning wines with our club members, we are off on our next adventure to share our winemaking traditions with the world.

TASTING ROOM INFORMATION: By appointment only; new tasting room hours to be announced.

DIRECTIONS: From I-70 at Exit #157 (Wolcott/Steamboat Springs): Turn right (north) off exit ramp; turn left (west) onto Hwy 6; turn right (north) onto Hwy 131. Continue on Hwy 131 for 4 miles to 4 Eagle Ranch, located on the right.

OTHER AMENITIES AT WINERY: Facility available for all event functions and has a restaurant onsite. During the summer, horseback riding, cattle round-ups, zip line tours, rafting, rock climbing and a petting zoo are available. During the winter months enjoy snowmobiling, dogsled adventures and sleigh rides.

WINE AVAILABLE FOR PURCHASE OUTSIDE OF WINERY: No

OTHER TASTING ROOM LOCATIONS: No

NOTES: _____

_____

_____

_____

WINTER PARK WINERY

395 Zerex Street, Fraser, CO 80442
970-726-4514
winterparkwinery.com
jon@winterparkwinery.com

OWNER: Jon Brickner

YEAR BEGAN OPERATION: 2004

AVERAGE CASES PRODUCED ANNUALLY: 1,000

WINES PRODUCED:
White: Chardonnay, Riesling, White Zinfandel
Red: Cabernet Sauvignon, Merlot, Syrah
Other: Blend called Grateful Red; Port wine

MESSAGE FROM OWNER: Located in downtown Fraser along US Hwy 40, the Winter Park Winery prides itself on its wine, small town charm and great atmosphere. Like the wine, it offers a bold, rich and flavorful spice to the local community, and invites locals and visitors alike to come and experience the festivities. All of our wines are made onsite and are handcrafted to achieve the best quality red and white wines. All of our wine is unfiltered to maintain full-mouth feel and flavor, while keeping all of the nutrients wine has to offer.

In addition to our wines, we also have the Winter Park Winery Bike Team, which competes in sport, expert and pro categories. Be sure to check our website frequently or sign-up for our "ezine" to hear about specials, music and events happening at the winery!

TASTING ROOM INFORMATION: Daily, from 12:30 to 6 p.m.; May and November by appointment.

DIRECTIONS: Located in downtown Fraser, which is just north of Winter Park, on Hwy 40 (Zerex Street).

OTHER AMENITIES AT WINERY: N/A

WINE AVAILABLE FOR PURCHASE OUTSIDE OF WINERY: No

OTHER TASTING ROOM LOCATIONS: No

NOTES: _____

_____

_____

_____

MOUNTAINS REGION
What Else To See & Do

The Mountains Region covers a vast amount of area with numerous things to see and do in the cities and counties that encompass the central Rockies. Below is a small sampling of activities and locations. See the Internet for further information. Current Colorado wineries/tasting rooms in the region are located in the following cities: Bailey, Breckenridge, Conifer, Fairplay, Georgetown, Glenwood Springs, Minturn, Redstone and Winter Park.

Aspen   aspenchamber.org/stayaspensnowmass.com

Georgetown   georgetown-colorado.org

Georgetown Train   georgetownlooprr.com
Let the journey begin as you travel from Silver Plume down 600' to Georgetown and back. When completed in 1884, the route was considered an engineering marvel. Reservations highly recommended.

Ghost Towns   ghosttowns.com/states/co/co.html
How did the town become established? Who lived there? Why did they leave? Colorado is teeming with ghost towns packed with western history.

Glenwood Springs   visitglenwood.com

Grand County   visitgrandcounty.com

Hot Springs   trails.com
Need to soak and relax after all your wine tasting? Try one of Colorado's 50+ hot springs located throughout the state. Trails.com has the entire list, so check out the website before you travel into any Wine Region. Here are just a few:
- Cottonwood Hot Spring & Inn   cottonwood-hot-springs.com
- Glenwood Hot Springs   hotspringspool.com
- Indian Hot Springs   indianhotsprings.com
- Mt Princeton Hot Springs Resort   mtprinceton.com
- Strawberry Park Hot Springs   strawberryhotsprings.com
- The Springs Resort & Spa   pagosahotsprings.com

Leadville
leadville.com

Maroon Bells
aspenchamber.org

The Maroon Bells are considered to be the most photographed peaks in Colorado. Any season of the year provides breathtaking scenery.

Mine tours
colorado.com/Mines.aspx

"Is there any more gold in them thar hills?" Learn about Colorado's mining history and see where prospectors spent their time. There are a variety of mine tours throughout the Mountain Region. Here are just a few:

- Breckenridge — countryboymine.com
- Georgetown — georgetownlooprr.com
- Idaho Springs — phoenixgoldmine.com / historicargotours.com

Minturn
minturn.org

Mount Evans
mountevans.com

Ever been to the top of North America's highest paved auto road? Drive to the top of Mount Evans (elevation 14,264') for the experience of a lifetime, as you pass through several ecosystems and glimpse the state animal (Rocky Mountain Bighorn Sheep).

Outdoor Activities

Winter, Spring, Summer or Fall the Rocky Mountains have it all! Whatever your interests or abilities, the Mountain Region provides incredible outdoor enjoyment.

- Cross-Country Skiing and Snowshoeing — trails.com / individual city & county websites
- Fishing — wildlife.state.co.us/FISHING
- Hiking and Biking — 14ers.com / trails.com / individual city & county websites
- Rafting — colorado.com/WhitewaterRafting.aspx
- Skiing / Boarding (downhill) — coloradoski.com

Park County
parkco.us

Redstone Castle
redstonecastle.us

There is a castle in Colorado? Yes, built in 1897 for coal and steel magnate John Cleveland Osgood.

Summit County   **summitchamber.org**
- Breckenridge   gobreck.com
- Copper Mountain   coppercolorado.com
- Dillon   townofdillon.com
- Frisco   townoffrisco.com
- Keystone   keystone.travel
- Silverthorne   silverthorne.org

Winter Park   **winterparkgov.com**

Vail   **vail.com**

MOUNTAINS REGION
Additional Tasting Locations

Canyon Wind Cellars Tasting Room (Anemoi Wines and Canyon Wind Cellars)
1500 Argentine Street, Georgetown, CO 80444
303-569-3152
canyonwindcellars.com
Owner: Jay and Jennifer Christianson
Hours: Daily, from 10 a.m. to 6 p.m.

Coyote Creek Studio Arts (DeBeque Canyon Winery)
419 Front Street, Fairplay, CO 80440
719-836-2040
coyotecreekarts.com
Owner: Artist Co-op
Hours: Daily, from 10 a.m. to 5 p.m.

D'Vine Wine - Breckenridge (D'Vine Wine, Home of Wild Women Wine)
211 S. Main Street, Breckenridge, CO 80424
970-453-3991
winerydenver.com
Owner: Charlene and Ross Meriweather
Hours: Sunday, Tuesday through Thursday from noon to 6 p.m., Friday and Saturday from noon to 9 p.m.

Redstone Company Store (5680' Vineyards, Alfred Eames Cellars and Black Bridge Winery)
117 Redstone Boulevard, Redstone, CO 81623
970-963-3408
redstonecompanystore.com
Owner: Deb McCormick
Hours: varies

**The Chocolate Moose & Ice Cream Parlor
(Bookcliff Vineyards)**
710 Grand Avenue, Glenwood Springs, CO 81601
970-945-2723
website: n/a
Owner: John Garlich and Ulla Merz
Hours: varies

REFERENCES

Colorado Wine Industry Board. *Colorado: a Beautiful State of Wine.* 2011. Print.

Fay, Abbott. *The Story of Colorado Wine*s. First. Montrose, CO: Western Reflections Publishing Company, 2002.

Hawkins, Anthony. "Glossary of Wine Tasting Terminology." 1.4. (1995): n.pag. Web. November, 2011. http://zebra.sc.edu/smell/wine_glossary.html.

Marshall, Wes. *What's A Wine Lover To Do?*. First. New York, NY: Artisan, a division of Workman Publishing Company, Inc., 2010.

McCarthy, Ed, Mary Ewing-Mulligan, and Maryann Egan. *Wine All-In-One For Dummies*. First. Hoboken, NJ: Wiley Publishing, Inc., 2009.

Smith, Alta and Brad. *The Guide to Colorado Wineries*. Second. Golden, CO: Fulcrum Publishing, 2002.

Walton, Stuart. *Cook's Encyclopedia of Wine*. First. New York, NY: Barnes & Noble, Inc., 2005

Wikipedia. November 2012. http://en.wikipedia.or.

"Wine Facts." *Beekman Wines & Liquors* (1996): n.pag. Web. 3 Feb 2012. http://www.beekmanwine.com/factsquotes.htm.

"Wine Grapes." *Keep Wine Simple* (2008): n.pag. Web. November 2012. http://www.keepwinesimple.com/index.html.

Zraly, Kevin. *Windows On The World / Complete Wine Course*. First. New York, NY: Sterling Publishing, 2009.

LOCAL REFERENCES

Colorado Wine Industry Board

In 1977 the Colorado General Assembly enacted the Colorado Limited Winery Act to permit small "farm wineries", which paved the way for more commercial wineries to open. By 1990, the industry had developed to the extent that the General Assembly passed the Colorado Wine Industry Development Act. This created the Colorado Wine Industry Development Board, under the authority of the Colorado Department of Agriculture.

The CWIDB is comprised of nine members, who represent a variety of wine-industry fields. They are appointed by the Governor and the position is voluntary. In general, the board oversees the excise tax revenues and the $0.01/liter tax from Colorado wineries. These funds are used for research and development (overseen by Colorado State University) and for the marketing and promotion of Colorado wines and grapes. Part of their marketing efforts is the *Colorado: A Beautiful State of Wine* pamphlet. For more information: *www.ColoradoWine.com*

Colorado Association for Viticulture and Enology

The Colorado Association for Viticulture and Enology (CAVE) is an association that exists to encourage and support enology and viticulture in Colorado. CAVE promotes the interests of Colorado grape growers and wineries in legislative and political matters,

provides a forum for the exchange of ideas and to disseminate current information pertaining to optimum winemaking and agriculture practices for vineyards in the area. CAVE seeks to establish contacts and relationships with other associations, both regional and statewide, to further development and growth of the industry.

Colorado Mountain Winefest and Colorado Urban Winefest are the fundraisers for CAVE, and all funds go toward education, seminars, research and equipment purchases to improve the grape growing and winemaking of Colorado wines. For more information: *www.CAVEOnline.org*

Colorado Viticulture Information and Data

Through the Colorado Agricultural Experiment Station (AES) and Colorado State University, you can find statistics on Colorado's grape growing activities and other viticulture practices.

The Western Colorado Research Center is part of the AES network and is located south of Grand Junction. Its vision is to meet emerging and recognized needs of the western Colorado agricultural community and attempt to overcome challenges, solve problems, and create opportunities within the region and beyond.

For additional information, visit their website:*www.colostate.edu/programs/wcrc/index.html*

Colorado Proud

Colorado Proud is a program of the Colorado Department of Agriculture, promotes food and agricultural products that are grown, raised or processed in Colorado.

Visit *www.ColoradoProud.org* to learn more.

INDEX

ACKNOWLEDGMENTS

I would first like to thank my husband, Jim. It was his information about a Colorado brewery guidebook that inspired me to create a book about Colorado's wineries. Thanks, Jim, for the constant support and guidance as I wrote the book. A very special thanks is extended to my two daughters, Allison and Mackenzie, who listened to my thoughts and encouraged me to pursue my dream.

My deepest gratitude goes to the following people who made the book come to life: Thanks to Nick Zelinger of NZ Graphics, whose creativity and expertise made this guidebook a thing of beauty. You were so easy to work with and your advice was invaluable. Thanks to my dear friend, Evonne Dunn, who meticulously read the book and offered her thoughts and opinions any time I asked. Thanks to my cousin, Sheila Paxton, who provided her wisdom and knowledge based on her 25 years teaching English. Thanks to Sandy Lardinois of JeWeL Publishing for her final review and punctuation efforts.

I also extend my appreciation to my friends and colleagues who thought this guidebook was an excellent idea and encouraged my efforts.

A special thank you is given to Debra Ray, owner of Desert Moon Vineyards, who provided the picture of the Book Cliff Mountains for the front cover, Jacob Helleckson of Stone Cottage Cellars, who provided the picture of the West Elk Mountains for the back cover and to Jim Cox, of JC Photography in Palisade, for the Grand Valley Region picture.

Thank you all for your assistance.

ABOUT THE AUTHOR

Paula Mitchell has combined her interest in wine and passion for Colorado into this guidebook. Since moving to Colorado in 1976, Paula has traveled all over the state visiting its incredible sites and experiencing its outdoor opportunities. Enjoying wine and wanting to learn more about her own state's wine production, she has explored its diverse wineries and discovered the many high-quality wines produced here. The purpose of her guidebook is to help others explore and discover Colorado's wineries, so they too can experience and savor Colorado wines!

Paula lives in the metro Denver area with her husband and two daughters. This is her first book.

For more information or to purchase the book, please contact the author through her website at *www.ExploringColoradoWineries.com.*